Matthew Cooke

(1761 – 1829)

Twelve Psalm Tunes

composed for the use of the church at North Mymms

(c.1790)

edited and introduced by Ian Cutts

Matthew Cooke

http://www.fast-print.net/bookshop

MATTHEW COOKE:
TWELVE PSALM TUNES COMPOSED FOR THE USE OF THE CHURCH AT NORTH MYMMS

ISBN: 978-178456-350-9

A catalogue record for this book is available from the British Library

Further copies can be ordered from any reputable bookseller or directly from http://www.fast-print.net/bookshop or, alternatively, by contacting the editor at iancutts@fastmail.fm or 6 Rasper Road, London, N20 0LZ

First published 2016 by
FASTPRINT PUBLISHING
Peterborough, England.

CONTENTS

Based on "Cary's New and Accurate Plan of London..." (1787)

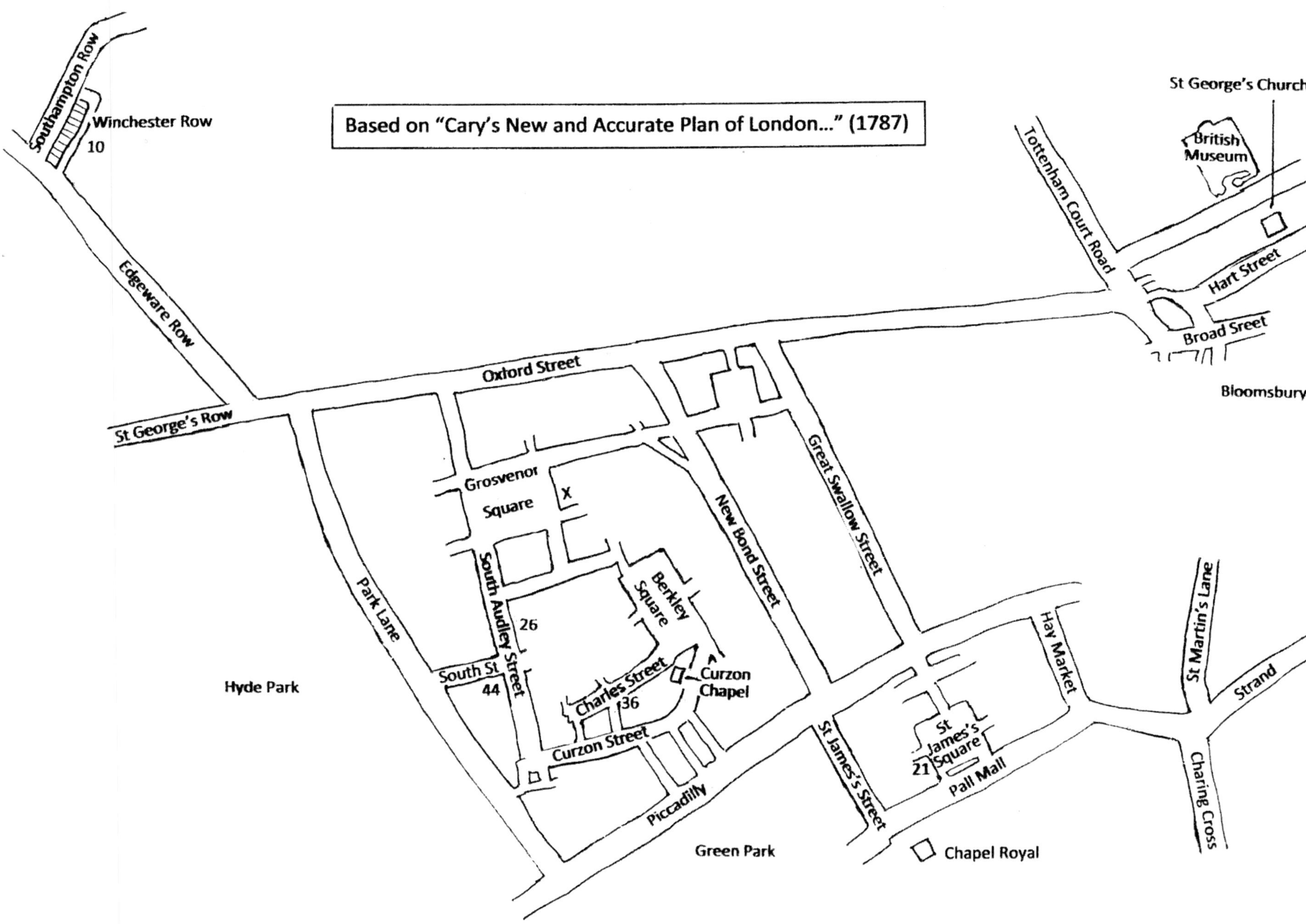

Introduction

Bosham Church

The Composer

Matthew Cooke was baptised on 21st December 1761, the sixth child of James and Mildred Cooke, who had ten years earlier moved from Brighton to Bosham, a village on the Sussex coast near Chichester, noted (in later years at least) for its flourishing church choir and band. His father was a sea captain; of his brothers and sisters, James was a baker, John followed his father (and in 1774 captained the ship which took Thomas Paine to America), Nathaniel was apprenticed to the steward of a local estate, Mildred emigrated to America, Jane died young, and Sarah married a navy surgeon.

The boy Matthew must have been an excellent singer, for he was entered into the choir of the Chapel Royal. The children of the Chapel Royal, ten in number, were often recruited from the provincial cathedrals, so Matthew may have sung in Chichester Cathedral choir, though this cannot be confirmed – his name does not appear among the choristers whose admissions and departures are recorded in the Cathedral's Act Books, but there are clear signs that the records are incomplete. The Chapel Royal children were housed, fed and clothed at the expense of the Crown, and were taught to read, write, to do arithmetic, sing, compose, and play on the organ or harpsichord. Cooke's master was James Nares, composer of church anthems and author of "A treatise on singing". He would also have encountered the elderly William Boyce, and he was acquainted with the young Thomas Linley, for whom he prepared many of the parts for the 1776 performance of Linley's "Ode on the Spirits of Shakespeare". In April 1777, his voice having broken, he left the Chapel Royal, taking with him the customary allowance of a set of clothes.

Some time after this, he became organist to the Countess Dowager of Essex, Lady Elizabeth Capel (nee Russell). She was the widow of William Capel, third Earl of Essex, whose family seat was at Cassiobury Park, near Watford. Probably Cooke's first published composition, in 1780 or shortly after, was "A sett of six lessons for the harpsichord or pianoforte", dedicated "with the utmost respect and gratitude" to Lady Elizabeth, and the subscription list suggests that she had persuaded many of her family and friends to order copies, as well as ordering ten for herself. His former master James Nares had published a similar set of lessons in 1747.

LIST OF SUBSCRIBERS

The Right Honble LADY AILESFORD.
Mr AYRTON, Mafter of the Children of his Majefty's Chapel Royal

Mrs BLAIR, Portland Place 2 Books
OLDFIELD BOWLES, Efq:

The Right Honble LADY DIANA CAPEL.
The Right Honble LADY ANN CAPEL.
The Countefs of CLARENDON
The Countefs of CORK and ORRERY.
The Right Honble LADY CRAVEN.
Sr JERVIS CLIFTON, Bart
The Revd Mr WILLIAM COLE, of Ely

THOMAS SANDERS DUPUIS Efq: Organift and compofer of his Majeftys Chapels Royal
Mr WILLIAM DALE.

The Countefs Dowager of ESSEX 10 Books
The Countefs of ESSEX
The Right Honble LADY CAROLINE EGERTON.

The Right Honble LADY MARY FORBES.
Mifs [illegible] FORBES.
Mifs Maria FORBES.
LADY FETHERSTONE.

The Right Honble LADY GRIMSTON.
The Right Honble Vifcountefs HOWE, 2 Books

ROBERT HALIFAX, Efqr
Mifs MARY HUDSON, St Peters HILL.
The Revd Mr HEILD, Kenfington

The Honble Mrs St IOHN.

THOMAS LINLEY, Efqr
Mr IOHN LUTHER.

The Right Honble LADY MONSON.
The Honble Mifs THEODOSIA MONSON.
The Right Honble LORD MALDEN.

His Excellency Baron NOLCKEN, ENVOY Extraordinary from the Court of SWEDEN.

Mrs POYNTZ 2 Books

The Right Honble the Earl of SANDWICH.
The Countefs of SALISBURY.
Mrs SNOW.

Sr IOHN TREVELYAN, Bart

THOMAS VINCENT, Efqr

The Right Honble LADY BETTY WORSLEY.
Mr JAMES WRIGHT.
Mr SAMUEL WEBBE.

The subscription list of "A sett of six lessons for the harpsichord or piano forte", c.1780

At about the same time he published three songs, two of them anonymously with only his initials, followed in 1782-4 by "A set of country dances as performed at the Grove, the seat of the Earl of Clarendon in Hertfordshire". The Grove was the neighbouring estate to Cassiobury Park, and the Earl of Clarendon was the husband of one of William Capel's daughters, by his first wife. In 1787 Matthew Cooke had a poem of his published in the Morning Herald, giving his address as "Russell Farm, Hertfordshire". Russell Farm was a dower house adjacent to Cassiobury Park, occupied by the Dowager Countess and her unmarried daughters Ann and Diana Capel. Cooke was therefore their resident musician. One of the dances is entitled "The Charms of Watford", and indeed the whole area, along the River Gade, was a renowned beauty spot. The family had also a house in London, at 36 Charles Street, Mayfair.

After the Dowager's death in 1784, Ann and Diana Capel retained Cooke as organist and "musician", and by 1788 he was lodging with them at Charles Street. It was shortly after this that he published the "Twelve psalm tunes composed for the use of the church at North Mims", dedicated to Francis Osborne, fifth Duke of Leeds, whose father had been a friend of William Capel.

MR COOKE

PROFESSOR of MUSIC,

(N° 36)

Charles Street Berkeley Square.

Most respectfully informs the NOBILITY, and GENTRY that He gives instructions on

The ORGAN, HARPSICHORD, PIANO-FORTE, and SINGING.

Private Concerts, and Select Parties attended on Evenings.

All kinds of Musical Instruments by the most eminent Makers purchased by Commis-sion for Exportation.

36 Charles Street, Mayfair (with flags) – the house numbers have not changed, and a page from "Select portions of the Psalms of David", c. 1795

© The British Library Board, C.16.z

St George's Church, Bloomsbury

In 1788 he obtained the post of organist at St George's, Bloomsbury, which up till then had had no organ, by offering to pay for an organ in return for being appointed organist for life, with no salary apart from voluntary contributions by the parishioners. This arrangement was accepted, but, predictably, the voluntary contributions became less generous year by year, and Cooke was at length forced to ask for a salary. It was not until 1798, after much negotiation, that the vestry finally agreed to pay him a permanent salary of £50 a year, to include maintenance costs, the organ having cost him personally £500. It was a 3-manual, 20-stop organ built by Henry Holland. His feelings cannot have been improved by the visit of Henry Leffler, who in his c.1800 survey of London organs described it as "a very bad organ". Still, the enterprise did ultimately work to Cooke's advantage, since he kept the job until his death in 1829, and even managed to get a pay rise out of them. For a short period around 1795, he was also organist at the Curzon Chapel, Mayfair, now demolished, and in that year he published "Select portions of the Psalms of David", a collection of congregational psalm tunes, some of them composed by him and others arranged by him. Cooke deputised as organist at the Lock Hospital chapel on various occasions from 1807 to 1809, and in 1808 published "A collection of psalm and hymn tunes for the use of the Lock Hospital Chapel", after the Hospital had first granted and then withdrawn permission for the dedication. It includes a hymn setting dedicated to William Wilberforce "by whose efforts the Slave Trade was abolished March 25th 1807". In 1822 the organist J S Holmyard published a collection of music "sung at the Episcopal Chapel of the London Society for promoting Christianity amongst the Jews", containing a large number of tunes and pieces by Cooke, among them some set pieces in Hebrew, and a hymn tune named "Bozham", after his native village. In all, Cooke composed at least 50 hymn tunes. He also composed some 35 songs and glees, some of which were performed in front of royalty, and a number of short pieces for keyboard, including some arrangements of waltzes, and in 1822 a set of quadrilles, dedicated to Mrs Berkeley Paget, whose husband was descended from the Capel family for whom he had worked in the 1780s.

As well as performing, teaching, composing and arranging, Cooke was a copyist, and the British Library holds his handwritten copies of William Linley's comic opera "The Pavilion" and Thomas Linley's "Ode on the Spirits of Shakespeare" – huge volumes which must have occupied many hours of painstaking work, carried out in 1798 and 1812 respectively, apparently for his own satisfaction rather than in connection with a performance. The second of these ends with Cooke's appreciation of the composer, lamenting his untimely death in a boating accident ("Oh! lost too early!!!"). He described Thomas Linley's "Song of Moses" as containing "the finest specimens in the simple, affecting, grand and sublime styles that was ever produced by the pen of a musician". He also admired Samuel Wesley, in particular on account of Wesley's "bringing forward the stupendous compositions of Sebastian Bach", as he put it. As a teacher, he deputised for Wesley during the latter's absences. Wesley in his letters described Cooke as "a most able Master and excellent Musician", and "a professional Man of real Worth and Talents (who is now my Assistant at another School)". On one occasion, Wesley, having outstayed his leave of absence, wrote that "Mrs Barnes, upon my Arrival in Town, expressed the highest Approbation of Mr Cooke's Attention and Punctuality," and Wesley could not understand why he himself was promptly sacked by Mrs Barnes.

In 1812 he was awarded the Gold Medal of the Society of Arts "for his invention of an apparatus by means of which blind people can both learn and teach music" – a system of brass characters pressed into a cushion, to be read by touch. He also advertised as a music teacher to the blind.

Some time after 1795, he left his lodgings at 36 Charles Street. An advertisement dated 1798 printed his address as 48 South Street, but this seems to have been an error, since the houses only went up to number 44. By May of 1800 he was at 26 South Audley Street, which in 1790 was recorded as an apothecary's shop, so Cooke presumably rented a room over the shop. Finally, from late 1804 until his death, he lived at 10 Winchester Row, Paddington, a terrace of rather small houses on the south side of today's Old Marylebone Road. By this time he had married an Elizabeth; they had a short-lived son, Matthew, who was buried on 20th January 1805. Elizabeth was buried on 10th May 1817, and six months later Matthew married another Elizabeth. They had another son Matthew, baptised on 19th July 1822, who, like his father, sang in the choir of the Chapel Royal, and went on to become an organist and songwriter, and also a prominent freemason. He in turn married an Elizabeth, and had a son called Matthew.

Matthew the first had a nephew Nathaniel, one of twins born to his older brother James and baptised on 9th May 1774. Nathaniel studied with his uncle Matthew in London, became organist of Brighton church, and published a collection of psalm tunes, mostly his own compositions. He died in April 1827 and was buried in the chancel of Bosham church, where there is a memorial.

Matthew Cooke was buried at St Mary's Church, Paddington Green, on 7th June 1829, aged 67. His grave stone (if any) seems to have become illegible by the time the burial ground was surveyed in 1888. In March 1830, his widow was forced to appeal to the Royal Philharmonic Society for help, on account of "the destitute situation in which she is left and the privations she has endured during the past very severe winter".

The Dedicatee

The dedicatee of the *Twelve Psalm Tunes* was the owner of North Mymms Park, Francis Godolphin Osborne, fifth Duke of Leeds, known as Marquess of Carmarthen before inheriting his father's title in 1789. As well as North Mymms Park, he owned, but did not occupy, Godolphin in Cornwall, now owned by the National Trust, and Kiveton Park (the family seat) and Aston Manor in Yorkshire. He had two London addresses: 21 St James's Square, Westminster, and an un-numbered house on the east side of Grosvenor Square. He entered politics in 1774 and rose to become Foreign Secretary in 1783 in the government of William Pitt the Younger. He resigned in April 1791 after a disagreement with Pitt, and thereafter took little active part in politics.

He was born in 1751 into a music-loving family - his father, the fourth Duke of Leeds, was a great friend and patron of Farinelli, the most famous castrato singer of the age, and he himself also visited Farinelli when touring Italy in 1769-70. In 1773 he married Lady Amelia D'Arcy, with the encouragement of his father, who had unsuccessfully courted Amelia's aunt, Lady Caroline Darcy. However, in 1779 she eloped with Captain John Byron, nicknamed "Mad Jack". After the divorce, Amelia married the captain, but died a few years later; the captain re-married and went on to father Lord Byron the poet, famously described as "mad, bad and dangerous to know" – obviously, enduring family characteristics.

Carmarthen (as he was still) re-married in 1788. His new wife, Catherine Anguish, "chiefly attracted the attention of his Grace by her peculiar taste and skill in musick", according to his obituary in *The Gentleman's Magazine*. Lady Mary Coke commented, "The lady is not handsome but is a perfect mistress of music…I cannot say I admire her; there is the appearance of good humour but her manner is vulgar." On April 15th 1791, the Duke recorded, "in the evening there was a concert at Lady Holdernesse' in order that their Majesties might hear the Miss Anguishs sing. The King, Queen, and five of the Princesses were there…" It is quite likely that his acquaintance with Matthew Cooke came about through music lessons, since Cooke gave instruction to the nobility and gentry, and the two men lived a short distance apart; furthermore the Duke's father had been a friend of William Capel, husband of Cooke's former employer the Countess Dowager of Essex and father of Ann and Diana Capel.

The Duke and Duchess visited Godolphin briefly in June 1791 and never went there again. They inherited 21 St James's Square from the fourth Duke in 1789, and had it rebuilt 1790–93 with Robert Brettingham as architect. For one reason or another, the new house was found so unsatisfactory that plans were immediately made to demolish and rebuild again, this time with Soane as architect, though, in the event, Brettingham's house was only modified. Soane was employed again in 1797 for repairs and additions to North Mymms House.

Francis Godolphin Osborne, Fifth Duke of Leeds,
from an engraving after a portrait by Thomas Lawrence c.1792

The Misses Anguish, satirised by James Gillray in "Dilletanti Theatricals" (1803)

North Mymms Park, in a painting by George Sidney Shepherd published c.1820; and today

Of the several assessments of the Duke's character, the most reliable is probably that of Sir James Bland Burges, the man chosen by the Duke to be his under-secretary when in government:

"At the period to which I have just referred [1780-83]...his talents were brilliant and acute, his memory uncommonly retentive, his power of conception so prompt that he was able at a glance to comprehend whatever was submitted to him, and to decide upon the line of action to be taken; while his ready wit and his wonderful faculty of expression, whether by speech or by writing, in prose or in verse, charmed and dazzled all with whom he associated...In addition to all this, few equalled him in personal beauty of face and figure. His countenance was most prepossessing and seemed to indicate at once the quickness of his intellect and the suavity of his disposition. He had the gallant spirit of a noble gentleman with the manners and address of an accomplished courtier...No young man at that day was so generally admired, nor was there any one of whose future success a higher expectation had been formed...[However,] there were, indeed, many weaknesses, many blemishes, and much misconduct, which, perhaps, more than counterbalanced all his natural and acquired advantages, and which, as he advanced in life, sensibly lowered him in public estimation, and afforded a melancholy illustration of the insufficiency of rank, fortune, talents, and accomplishments to ensure happiness or good repute, while unsupported by discretion and uncontrolled by principle."

The King commented to Burges in 1793, "I know the Duke of Leeds well enough to be satisfied of his capricious and variable disposition," and in 1795, "Almost all our young men of fashion have been spoiled by the same thing – by having a parcel of dirty low toad-eaters about them, who poison their minds."

On the Duke's death in 1799, Joseph Farington wrote in his diary:

(1st February 1799) "Duke of Leeds died last night. Soane said He had lived freely lately, and drank a good deal of French wine."... (31st March 1799): Malone dined with the Duke of Leeds abt ten days before his death. The Duke constantly attended the Literary Club, where He talked rather too much, thereby engrossing the Conversation. Malone observed that He drank more wine than anybody there, perhaps three pints of Claret. He so often alluded to the situation he had filled of Secretary of State that it was joke to offer a wager "what time wd pass before the Duke [referred to] it by some allusion". He was too fond of low company, particularly that of Players, and talked too much of them and their concerns in high company which regarded them not. He kept late hours till 3 or 4 in the morning, and gamed, so as to distress Himself, which together caused him to be restless and uneasy...The Duke and Duchess, on account of his irregular mode of proceeding, were supposed not to be very comfortable together."

In 1799 his son, now the sixth Duke of Leeds, inherited North Mymms Park, and sold it in the same year. 21 St James's Square was also put up for sale in that year, and was eventually sold at a huge loss.

North Mymms Church, from an engraving by J Buckler, published c.1820; and today. The spire was erected 1806 – 11 and taken down in 1953

The Church

The Church of St Mary, North Mymms, Hertfordshire, stands at the end of a narrow lane, next to the old and new vicarages, half-a-dozen cottages, and North Mymms Park – now a management training centre. The church was built around 1340 by the then owners of the manor house, which was rebuilt in the late 16th century and was known variously as North Mymms Park, House or Place. The hamlet is surrounded by woods and fields. The settlement may once have been larger; the area is prone to flooding. The parish is a large one, and as well as the Park included the estates of Gubbins, Potterells, Skimpans, Muffats and Brookmans, making for a higher-than-average proportion of gentry among the parishioners. Today, the main population of the parish is in nearby Brookmans Park and Welham Green.

From "A topographical map of Hartford-Shire", by Andrew Dury and John Andrews 1766 (Hertfordshire Archives CM 26)

In the 18th century few country churches had organs, so voluntary choirs were formed, initially to lead congregational singing, but often proceeding to anthems and elaborate psalm settings not suitable for congregational singing. Instrumental support was at first limited to a bassoon or cello, but other string and wind instruments became commonplace in the later part of the century. The singers and players were mainly recruited from the traders, craftsmen, schoolteachers and so on. A large repertoire of music was composed and published for country choirs, some of it by the choir leaders themselves, who generally had little formal musical training, and some of it by town organists, who published their work with designations such as "calculated for country choirs" on the title pages. Itinerant music teachers trained the choirs and compiled books of psalms and anthems, often a mixture of their own compositions and those of others. John Ivery of Northaw – just five miles from North Mymms – published his collection "The Hertfordshire Melody" in 1773. As mentioned before, Cooke's home village of Bosham had a flourishing choir with – at some point - a band that included flute, clarinet, bassoon, two violins, and a cello made of copper. It is not certain when this choir came into being, but the Sussex Archaeological Society holds several music books that were used by the Bosham choir, bearing autographs dated from 1796 onwards. It is likely that this choir was in existence by the 1770s, as it is otherwise hard to account for Cooke's obvious excellence as a singer.

Usually referred to then as "the singers", these country choirs were not robed and did not sit in the chancel; sometimes they had their own pew at the back of the church, but frequently a gallery was erected for their use at the west end of the church, giving rise to the modern expressions "west gallery choir" and "west gallery music" (coined by Thomas Hardy). Experience of singing in church galleries by modern choirs specialising in this music has shown that this arrangement improves the singers' confidence and ensemble, and gives good projection into the church.

The gallery of Dorking Church

pen and ink drawing with wash by John Nixon, 1788 (private collection)

The gallery of North Mymms Church today.

At North Mymms a gallery was erected sometime after 1731; it is still there today. But, as the petition reproduced below shows, it was built to provide extra space, since "so great a part of the Parish Church…is now taken up by Pews appropriated to the Gentry…that there is not room sufficient for the Farmers and other Parishioners to kneel at Divine Worship and sit at Sermon in the Pews or Seats erected in the Body of the said Church." The churchwarden's account book records payments for "beer for the ringers", but makes no mention of singers, nor of instruments or spare strings or reeds. The existence of Cooke's "Twelve psalm tunes (in four parts) composed for the use of the church at North Mims" strongly suggests that there was a choir – the pieces are certainly not suitable for congregational singing – and it must have been a competent choir, assuming they did actually succeed in singing the pieces. They may have been trained by John Ivery, unless Cooke started a choir from scratch. It is likely, too, that they sat in the gallery, as this was the usual place for a choir at that time. Psalm 33 has parts for bassoon and oboe, Psalm 105 for bassoon only, from which it may be assumed that players of those instruments were available, at least on some occasions.

To the very Revd —— Lunn D.D Archdeacon of Huntington, and to the Worl John Andrew LLD his Commissary and Official

Whereas so great a part of the Parish Church of North Mymms in the County of Hertford & Archdeaconry of Huntington is now taken up by Pews appropriated to the Gentry of the said Parish, that there is not room sufficient for the Farmers and other Parishioners to kneel at Divine Worship & sit at Sermon in the Pews or Seats erected in the Body of the said Church; Therefore the Vicar & Churchwardens of the said Parish do humbly petition, that a Faculty or Licence may be granted to erect a Gallery in the west End of the said Church of 19 foot breadth in front & 12 foot breadth in that part which is to be joined to the Belfry, and of 12 foot depth from the Belfry into the Church for the necessary Use of ye Parishioners pursuant to an Order of Vestry made for that purpose

John Alkin Vicar

Tho: Mathews his T Mark
Wm Edwards
Churchwardens

A petition from the churchwardens of St Mary's Church, North Mymms, to the Archdeacon of Huntington (sic), 1731 (Hertfordshire Archives AHH 19/1)

Extracts from the churchwarden's account book for North Mymms, from 1762 to 1907
(Hertfordshire Archives D/P 69/5/1)

There are references to "beer for the ringers" and "ringing days", but no mention of singers or instruments. The first mention of an organ or organist is in 1793.

1793 "Money received by rates and subscriptions in the office of church warden in the parish of Northmims towards defraying the expenses of the church and the organ"

By a rate in 1786	£66.13.3
By subscription	
His Grace the Duke of Leeds	21.6.0
(4 others, lesser amounts)	_______
	£53.11.00
1793 *continued...*	
Paid Mr Grundler Playing Organ	17.10.0
Mr Cooke D__ D__	128.12.6
1796	
(The Duke of Leeds paid another £21)	
Mr Grundler Playing organ	17.10.0
Mr Cooke D	128.12.6
1800 Paid Bills to Mess Hill, Cooke, Grundler, Hardum	183.16.8 ½
1817 printing psalm books for the church	11. 9.4
1820 paid Bundy for Organ Handle and Chimney Cowl	3.6
1820 Thomas Peck playing organ 52 weeks	5. 0.0
1821 Peck playing organ	5. 0.0
1823 Hudson playing organ	5. 0.0

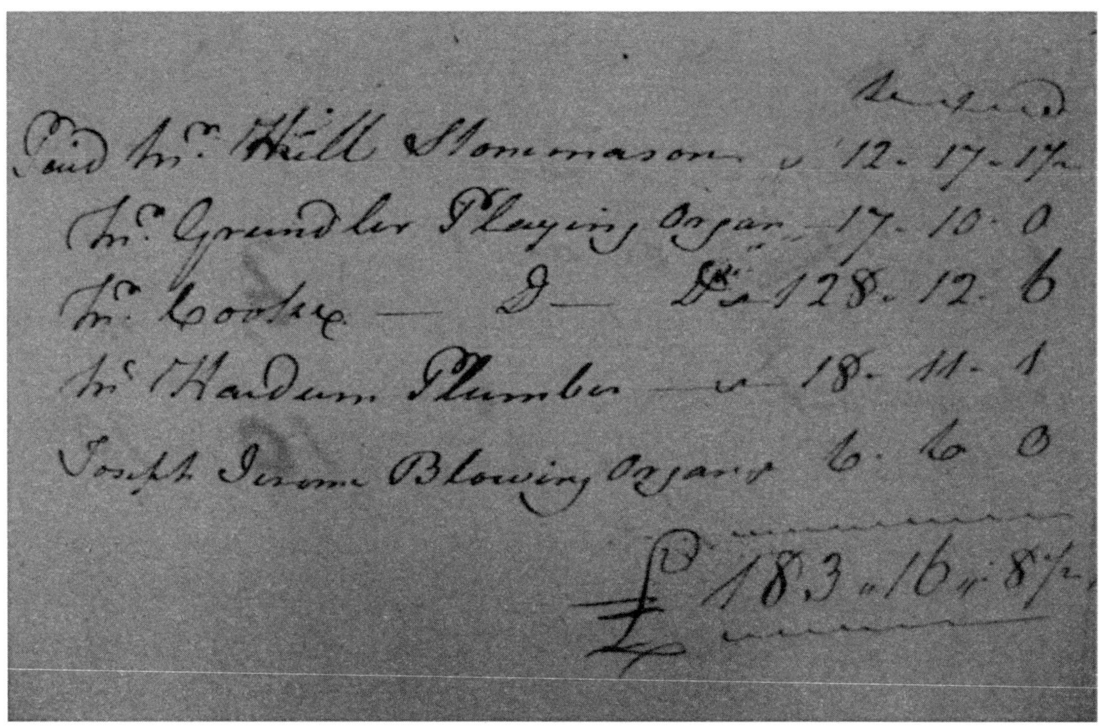

Paid Mr. Hill Stonemason — 12. 17. 1½
Mr. Grundler Playing Organ — 17. 10. 0
Mr. Cooke — D° — D° 128. 12. 6
Mr. Hadam Plumber — 18. 11. 1
Joseph Jerome Blowing Organs 6. 6. 0
£183. 16. 8½

A page from the churchwarden's account book of North Mymms Church, 1793 (Hertfordshire Archives D/P 69/5/1)

The first mention of an organ or organist in the account book is an entry for 1793, recording the sum of £128.12s 6d paid to Mr Cooke for "playing organ", compared with just £17.10s for the less fortunate Mr Grundler who was also paid for "playing organ". Subsequent entries suggest that this represented three years' worth of payments, which in turn suggests that an organ was installed around 1790. It is not known where this organ was situated at the time, but a church plan of 1859, the year of a major restoration, shows a small organ in the north aisle, with "children's seats" nearby. It was common practice in Georgian town churches for the singing to be led by children with organ accompaniment, and this was the case at Bloomsbury, so this arrangement may have been introduced at North Mymms, either in Cooke's time or at a later date. That the Duke and/or Duchess were responsible for Cooke's appointment at North Mymms can hardly be doubted, and Cooke's name disappears from the account book after the Duke's death in 1799. The couple seems to have begun to spend more time at North Mymms in the 1790s – their London house was being rebuilt, and the Duke resigned his cabinet post in April 1791. The Duke's surviving correspondence supports this assumption, and further confirmation is provided by a tablet in the church commemorating the man employed as tutor to the Duke's sons until the year 1794. It may also be relevant that a new vicar arrived in November 1790. The account book does not record the organ's purchase, so it may have been provided by the Duke, perhaps transferred from either North Mymms House or 21 St James's Square, where the rebuilding work had begun.

The north aisle of North Mymms Church, in a plan dated 1859, showing the position of the organ.

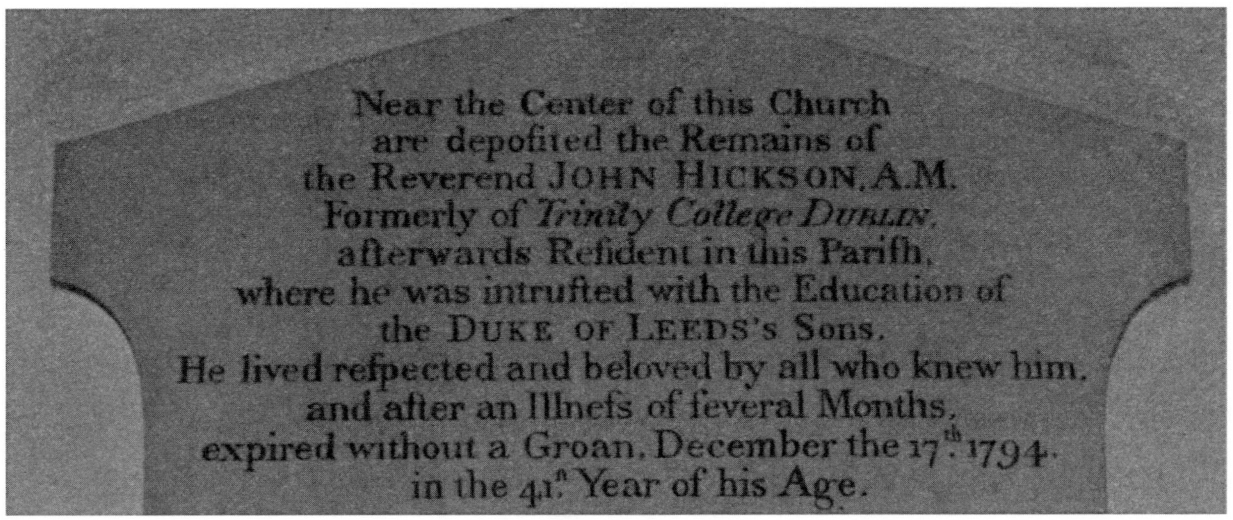

A tablet in North Mymms Church

On the title page of the *Twelve Psalm Tunes* Cooke describes himself as "Organist of North Mims, Hertfordshire, of St Georges, Bloomsbury London and Musician to the Right Honble the Ladies Capell". This raises the question: how did he hold down two posts as organist at once, in two places twenty miles apart? North Mymms is just one-and-a-half miles from the old Great North Road, and stage coaches from London could reach the area in around two-and-a-half hours. He might even have walked: Samuel Wesley was at this time living in the nearby parish of Ridge, walking the eighteen miles to his work in Marylebone, and sometimes returning the same day. As explained above, Cooke's position at Bloomsbury was initially a semi-voluntary one, so in principle he could give himself a week off when he wanted. In 1792, the vestry at Bloomsbury agreed to pay him a salary (later rescinded) "upon condition that he shall constantly play the Organ himself during the whole of the Winter season, and at other times employ a good performer in his stead". The concurrent payments to Grundler at North Mymms support the idea that Cooke was sometimes in London and sometimes at North Mymms. He placed an advertisement in *The Times* on 17th March 1798 for his collection "Divine Psalmody" (a reprint of his "Select Portions of the Psalms of David" of c.1795), claiming that "this work will prove of the greatest utility to young Practitioners in general, and Country Organists in particular, whose knowledge in Music does not extend to Thorough Bass, as the Chords are written to every Note, by which method the most unskilful performer may execute the same with the greatest facility". Presumably, one of the "unskilful country organists" he had in mind was Grundler, and the book was compiled partly with a view to its use at North Mymms.

Cooke was paid off in 1800, and no more payments were made to organists for the next 20 years. Payments for "playing organ" resumed in 1820, after a payment was made for an "organ handle". By this time the instrument in question was a barrel organ – possibly the same instrument with the addition of a barrel mechanism, or more likely a different instrument, the previous one having perhaps been sold to help clear the Duke's debts, whose property it may have been. The situation in the intervening twenty years is uncertain.

Twelve

PSALM TUNES,

in four Parts

Composed for the Use of the Church,

at NORTH MIMS;

& with the utmost Respect Dedicated to the most

Noble PRINCE Francis,

Duke of Leeds: &c. &c. &c.

BY

Matthew Cooke,

Organist of North Mims, Hertfordshire,

of St. Georges, Bloomsbury London

and Musician to the Right Honble. the Ladies Capell.

LONDON.

Printed for the Author by Henry Holland, at his Music Warehouse St. James's Street Piccadilly.

The Music

There are copies of the Twelve Psalm Tunes in the British Library and in the library of the Royal College of Music. There is no organ part, nor is the bass line figured, which is surprising, as Cooke describes himself on the title page as "organist of North Mims, Hertfordshire". The absence of anything indicating the use of an organ suggests that Cooke led or directed the choir in these pieces, and reserved the organ for congregational psalms and voluntaries; alternatively, it is possible that they were written for the choir before the organ was acquired, and published for the general market at a later date, after the arrival of the organ in about 1790. The book was "printed for the author by Henry Holland, at his Music Warehouse St James's Street Piccadilly"; this address is recorded as pertaining to the years 1789 – 93. The dedication to "Prince Francis, Duke of Leeds" confirms this, since that title was inherited in 1789.

It is intriguing that there are *twelve* psalm tunes (plus two Christmas hymns at the end), and the intention may have been to introduce them at a rate of one a month, perhaps to coincide with monthly visits. The particular psalms chosen, however, do not correspond to a consistent pattern among the daily psalms prescribed in the church lectionary, and they may have been chosen for their content, being in most cases concerned with praise. Of the two Christmas hymn texts, the second, "While shepherds watched their flocks by night" (Nahum Tate's metrical version of Luke chapter II verses 8 to 14), was widely sung in parish churches, to a wide variety of tunes. It had not yet become attached to "Winchester Old", the usual tune today. The other Christmas hymn, "The day spring from on high with lustre bright", is a rarity - there are no other settings in the Hymn Tune Index. The words are selected from a poem by Ann Murry published in 1779, and quote from Luke chapter I verse 78, and Psalm 65.

Cooke's former master at the Chapel Royal, James Nares, composed three anthems intended for country choirs, requiring "only a bassoon or other bass accompaniment", published posthumously in 1788 with an anonymous preface:

"…Concerning those three anthems in this set, which are calculated to be performed without an organ, the Author expressed himself to this effect, in a paper written in 1782. "Having often been an auditor in country churches, where what they called anthems were sung in parts, I own I have been usually mortified by the performance, though at the same time I pitied the performers; who had against them not only their own inexperience, but the badness of the music. Nor could I help observing, that the same time and pains bestowed upon some easy music, composed in a good style, would have produced an effect much more creditable to the singers, as well as more pleasing to the audience. I was therefore desirous to remedy in some degree this defect, and to supply a few pieces, which might be at the same time within the reach of those performers, and not wholly unworthy the attention of the more enlightened part of the congregation."

The music of country choirs, though far from primitive, could be somewhat rough and ready, both in the musical writing and in its execution, and today this is part of its appeal for many enthusiasts. But there were others besides Nares who sought to "improve" it, and Cooke may have been engaged by the Duke with this aim in mind. Metrical versions of the psalms formed the main musical content of worship in parish churches, but whereas in town churches only plain tunes were used, suitable for congregational singing, country choirs delighted in more elaborate settings, often with fugal passages. Cooke was thus writing in the style with which he was probably familiar from his childhood in Bosham. His later training shows itself in a number of ways: the melody is in the treble voice, whereas in country psalmody it was usually in the tenor at this time; his harmonic.

14

PSALM XXXIII.

writing is particularly effective, and tends to favour inverted chords; many of the pieces give prominence to the alto voice; appoggiaturas are used liberally; and the tenor part is written in the tenor clef, rarely seen in music intended for country choirs. Rather old-fashioned is the choice of the "Old Version" – Sternhold and Hopkins's metrical versions of the psalms, which by then were yielding popularity to the "New Version" of Tate and Brady. Most of the pieces are majestic in style, perhaps another echo of the Chapel Royal. Psalm 137 is singled out for treatment as an anthem (in the broader sense of a through-composed setting of either a metrical or a prose text, the sense in which the term was used by Nares). In his days at the Chapel Royal, Cooke may have sung in Boyce's anthem on this psalm, in the same key.

The pieces do not appear to have been widely disseminated. It was a period when such pieces were commonly reprinted in the publications of composers other than the original one, often many times over; but, although Cooke included the setting of "While shepherds watched" in his own collection "Select Portions of the Psalms of David", no others are known to have been reprinted in the years up to 1820 (the period currently covered by the Hymn Tune Index). The two Christmas hymns have been found in the notebooks of the folklorist Janet Blunt (1859-1950), who apparently copied them from a manuscript formerly used at Hook Norton, Oxfordshire (this manuscript has not been traced). Here, the last four bars of "While shepherds watched" and the last eight bars of "The day spring from on high" are repeated – a common practice among gallery choirs; in other respects they are exact copies of Cooke's original.

It will be noticed that the tenor and bass parts frequently cross, resulting in moments when the bass singers' note is apparently not the lowest note. This is hard to explain, since the soprano and alto parts never cross, and the part-writing is "correct" in other respects, so it can hardly have been a simple oversight on the part of the composer. Few English organs at that time had pedals (the Bloomsbury organ did not), so Cooke could hardly have intended the bass line to be played on a 16' organ stop since that would have affected the tenor part as well. Double basses were very rare in country church bands, though not unknown. The tenor voice, if it had instrumental support, was nearly always accompanied at treble pitch – violas were similarly rare in bands, as was the vox humana (an instrument similar to the cor anglais). As two of the pieces specify bassoon, it is probable that the reinforcement provided to the bass line by that instrument was thought sufficient to prevent the tenor part from dominating where it should not. The bassoon *could* have been played an octave below written pitch much of the time, but this would necessitate frequent jumping up and down octaves. In practice I have found that, with bassoon accompaniment at written pitch, the part-crossing is not a problem.

The high quality of these pieces makes it regrettable that Matthew Cooke composed relatively little other music.

Editorial policy

Only the first verse of each psalm is underlaid in the original; the second and third verses are given at the end of each piece. As often happens in elaborate strophic psalm settings with repeated phrases, the repetitions that work satisfactorily in the first verse do not work in the second and third verses, and it has been necessary to make editorial decisions on word-fit and on repetitions.

Cooke gave three verses for each of the strophic settings, with the exception of Psalm 33, which had four, and here I have omitted the original third verse since the word-fit was unsatisfactory. In Psalm 9, I have replaced the original verses 2 and 3, concerned with the destruction of enemies, with other lines from the same version of the psalm, which may be considered more suitable for present-day use. The original verses 2 and 3 were as follows:

Because my foes are driven back and turned unto flight/ They do fall down and are destroy'd by thy great pow'r and might./ Thou hast avenged all my wrong, my grief and all my grudge;/ Thou dost with justice hear my cause most like a righteous judge.

Thou dost rebuke the heathen folk, and wicked so confound,/ That afterwards the memory of them cannot be found. Destructions to an end are come, and cities overthrown;/ With them likewise are perished their fame and great renown.

Similarly, I have replaced the original third verse of Psalm 46 with other lines from the same version of the psalm. The original third verse was:

In midst of her the Lord doth dwell, she never.can decay/ All things against her that rebel, the Lord will surely slay./ The heathen folk and kingdoms fear, the people make a noise:/ The earth doth melt and disappear, when God puts forth his voice.

In the case of Psalm 48, I have removed the original second verse, put the original third verse in its place, and added a third verse from other lines of the same version of the psalm. The original second verse was:

Within the palaces thereof God is a refuge known;/ For lo, the Kings are gatherd, and together they are gone:/ But when they did behold it so, they wonder'd, and they were/ Astonish'd much and suddenly were driven back with fear.

The original spellings have been retained, except that in Psalm 137 bar 49, the spelling of "rais'd" has been altered to "raz'd". The original punctuation and capitalization was quite haphazard and has been rationalized.

The half-bar at bar 4 of Psalm 48 is in the original. Small notes in the bass part are suggested alternatives (except in Psalm 105); Cooke does not give bass notes below G.

With some misgivings I have changed the key of Psalm 9 and "While shepherds watched" from A to G, and that of Psalm 47 from E to Eb. This will ease matters for sopranos and tenors, and facilitate playing on Bb clarinet and serpent, instruments popular with the modern-day west gallery revival movement. I can supply these in the original keys on request, also versions for transposing instruments.

In other respects, the pieces are unaltered. Appogiaturas are left as given in the source, to allow for free interpretation. Beam groups are used as originally printed. The pieces are presented in the same order as in the original, that is, numerical order. I have avoided page turns, at the cost of some crowding. I recommend performance with instruments, ideally to include oboe and bassoon, but they may be performed with organ, or – except in the case of Psalm 33 – unaccompanied. Keyboard reductions are given at the end of the book, to reduce page-turning.

In most cases, a speed of around 80 crotchets per minute will give a suitably strong feel to the music

About the editor

Ian Cutts studied languages at Bradford University before beginning a career as a librarian, also becoming an active amateur musician. Now retired from librarianship, he has pursued musical studies at Benslow Music Trust, Cambridge Early Music and Morley College. He was director of the Chiltern West Gallery Quire from 1993 to 2010, and has carried out much research into the music of country choirs in Hertfordshire and Buckinghamshire.

Acknowledgements

Thanks are due to the following for permission to reproduce items in their care:

The British Library, for the subscription list on page 5, the advertisement on page 6, and the extracts from Cooke's book on pages 22 and 24.
Hertfordshire Archives and Local Studies, for the map on page 14, the petition on page 17, and the extract from the churchwarden's account book on page 19.
The print of the gallery of Dorking Church on page 15 is copied from the New Grove Dictionary of Music and Musicians, by permission of Oxford University Press. Attempts to trace the owner of the print have not been successful.
Other images are photographs taken by the author.

I wish also to thank the Reverend Sally Davenport, formerly vicar of St Mary's Church, North Mymms, for welcoming the performance of Cooke's music at the Snowdrop Sunday services held at the church from 2006 to 2010; and all members past and present of the Chiltern West Gallery Quire.

Sources

(given in the order in which they relate to the text)

Page 5 Bosham Parish Register, at West Sussex Record Office, Chichester

Ancestry Library www.ancestrylibrary.com

M Gowler: "Ellis memories". *Sussex Family Historian,* vol. 3 no. 6, September 1978, pp 171-172. A transcript of a family history written in 1864 by Josiah Ellis, grandson of Matthew Cooke's brother Nathaniel.

Sussex Record Society vol. 32: Sussex Marriage Licences: Archdeaconry of Chichester: 1771 October 7. W. Heffer 1926. This gives James the younger's occupation as baker; Josiah Ellis (above) says he became a brewer.

G B Keen: "Descendants of Jöran Kyn". *Pennsylvania Magazine of History and Biography,* vol. 4 no. 3, p 349.

John Keane: "Thomas Paine: a political life". Bloomsbury 1995

Page 6 Lord Chamberlain: Treasury: various entry books of warrants 1760-1819, p 282. National Archives ref. T 56/20

Chichester Cathedral Act Books, at West Sussex County Record Office, refs Cap. 1/3/4 and 1/3/5. These books give the names of choristers admitted, and the names of those they replaced. Cooke's name does not appear, but there are missing years, and departures without prior arrivals.

The Chapel Royal: the children and their masters", in "Office-holders in modern Britain" vol. 11 (revised), ed. R Bucholz. University of London 2006

J Doane: "A musical directory for the year 1794". Westley 1794

"Biographical Dictionary of actors, actresses, musicians, dancers, managers and other stage personnel in London 1660 – 1800", ed. Philip H Highfill and others, vol 3. Southern Illinois UP 1975. According to Highfill, Cooke "was listed in Doane's Musical Directory as a player on the tenor violin"; in fact the entry in Doane uses only the word "tenor", and it is clear from the other entries that tenor voice is meant.

§2 Matthew Cooke's employers are named on the title pages of his publications.

Page 7 John Edwin Cussans: "History of Hertfordshire: Hundred of Cashio". Chatto and Windus/Stephen Austin 1881

Robert Clutterbuck: "The histories and antiquities of the county of Hertford". John Nichols 1815-27

Morning Herald, 15th September 1787

John Hassell: "Picturesque rides and walks …thirty miles round the British Metropolis". J Hassell 1817

§2 A census of the parish of St George's, Hanover Square, taken in 1790; on microfilm at London Metropolitan Archives

Page 8 Vestry minutes of St George's Church, Bloomsbury, 1788 – 1801; on microfilm at Holborn public library

"The Leffler manuscript"; facsimile edition with introduction by Peter Williams. British Institute of Organ Studies 2010

Nicholas Temperley: "The Lock Hospital Chapel and its Music". *Journal of the Royal Musical Association,* vol. 118 no. 1 (1993) pp 61-62

J S Holmyard: "The psalms, hymns and miscellaneous pieces as sung at the Episcopal Chapel of the London Society for promoting Christianity amongst the Jews". J D Causton 1822. Holmyard was organist of the chapel from 1820; the society's archives (in the Bodleian Library) show that there were two others before him, but Cooke was not one of them.

Page 9 Gwilym Beechey: "Thomas Linley, Junior 1756-1778". *The Musical Quarterly,* no. 54, January 1968

Musica Britannica volume 30: Thomas Linley the younger: "Ode on the spirits of Shakespeare", edited by Gwilym Beechey; introduction. Stainer and Bell 1970

Gwilym Beechey: "Thomas Linley junior: his life, work and times". Unpublished Ph D thesis, University of Cambridge, 1964. Beechey suggests that Cooke had a lasting friendship with the Linley family, but does not really give any evidence for this.

Thomas Linley the younger: "An Ode on the Spirits of Shakespeare"; manuscript copy by Matthew Cooke 1812. British Library manuscript Egerton MS 2492

William Linley: "The Pavilion"; manuscript copy by Matthew Cooke. British Library Egerton MS 2494. The British Library has assigned the date 1796 to this (the year "The Pavilion" was produced), but the manuscript ends with the date 21st December 1798.

Unpublished "Impromptu" for organ by Matthew Cooke in imitation of J S Bach, in a collection of manuscripts presented to Vincent Novello. British Library manuscript Add MS 65488

Philip Olleson: "Samuel Wesley: the man and his music". Boydell 2003

"Letters of Samuel Wesley: professional and social correspondence 1797 – 1837", ed. Philip Olleson. Oxford UP 2001

§2 *Transactions of the Society, instituted in London, for the Encouragement of Arts, Manufactures, and Commerce*, vol. 30 (1813)

§3 Richard Horwood: "Plan of the Cities of London and Westminster", editions of 1794-9 and 1819; at London Metropolitan Archives. This map shows house numbers.

Rate books and 1821 Census for St Marylebone parish; on microfilm at Westminster City Archives

§4 "A Dictionary of Musicians from the earliest ages to the present time". Sainsbury and Co 1824

§5 Registers for St Mary's Paddington Green Churchyard and disused burial ground, c.1888-89; at Westminster City Archives

Royal Philharmonic Society manuscript 339 p.118. British Library RPS MS 339

Page 10 Oxford Dictionary of National Biography. Oxford UP

§2 Thomas McGeary: "Farinelli and the Duke of Leeds". *Early Music*, May 2002

The Gentleman's Magazine, February 1799 pp 168-9

"The Lovely Moralist: an epistle from a late unfortunate young lady to her lover The M-r-s of C-r-m". R. Faulder 1779

§3 Lady Mary Coke's manuscript journals, quoted in "Horace Walpole's Correspondence", ed. W S Lewis, vol 31. Yale UP/Oxford UP 1961

"Political memoranda of Prince Francis 5th Duke of Leeds". Camden Society 1882

§4 Osborne, 5th Duke of Leeds: "Tour to the West", 1791. British Library manuscript Add MS 28570

"Survey of London", vols 29 and 30: St James Westminster, Part 1 – South of Piccadilly. Athlone Press 1960

Dorothy Stroud: "Sir John Soane architect". Faber 1984

Page 13 "Selections from letters and correspondence of Sir James Bland Burges, Bart., sometime under-secretary of state for foreign affairs", ed. James Hutton. John Murray 1885

§5 "The Diary of Joseph Farington", ed. Kenneth Garlick and Angus Macintyre, vol 4. Yale UP 1979

Page 15 M R Hatfeld: "A short history of North Mymms Park". FANG Hatfield Publications 1998

Page 16 K H MacDermott: "Bosham Church: its history and antiquities". J W Moore 1911

K H MacDermott: "Sussex church music in the past". Moore and Wingham 1922

K H MacDermott: "The old church gallery minstrels". SPCK 1948

Page 18 A petition from the churchwardens of St Mary's Church, North Mymms to the Archdeacon of Huntington (sic), 1731; at Hertfordshire Archives and Local Studies

Churchwarden's account book for St Mary's Church, North Mymms, from 1762 to 1907; at Hertfordshire Archives and Local Studies

Page 20 A plan of St Mary's Church, North Mymms, dated 1859; on display in the church

Correspondence of the Dukes of Leeds, volumes 7 and 8. British Library manuscripts Add MS 28066 and 28067

Page 22 Suzan Carr: "Coaching days in Barnet". Barnet Libraries 1982

The Times 17th March 1798, page 2

§2 A bill dated 1831 for "repairing the organ in North Mims church resetting both barrels", in John Gray Accounts volume 1, British Organ Archive, Cadbury Research Library. The sum of £5 per year paid for "playing organ" from 1820 is consistent with barrel operation. (Information kindly supplied by Maggie Kilbey)

Page 24 Charles Humphries and William C Smith: "Music publishing in the British Isles". Blackwell 1970

§2 Nicholas Temperley and others: "The Hymn Tune Index". Oxford UP 1998; also online

Ann Murry: "Poems on various subjects". A Murry 1779

§3 James Nares: "A morning and evening service…together with six anthems in score". Preston 1788

Page 26 Notebooks of Janet Blunt, volume 15. Vaughan Williams Memorial Library shelfmark 10/10/13. Cited in "Oxfordshire Carols: 21 carols from Oxfordshire villages", ed. Dave Townsend. Serpent Press 2013

Psalm 9
Thomas Sternhold
Matthew Cooke
Soprano
With heart and mouth to thee, O Lord, will I sing laud and praise, And speak of all thy wond'-rous
Know thou that he who is a - bove for e - ver more shall reign: And in the seat of e - qui-
And they that know thy ho - ly Name, there - fore shall trust in thee: For thou for - sak-est not their
Alto
With heart and mouth to thee, O Lord, will I sing laud and praise, And speak of all thy wond'-rous
Know thou that he who is a - bove for e - ver more shall reign: And in the seat of e - qui-
And they that know thy ho - ly Name, there - fore shall trust in thee: For thou for - sak-est not their
Tenor
With heart and mouth to thee, O Lord, will I sing laud and praise, And speak of all,
Know thou that he who is a - bove for e - ver more shall reign: And in the seat,
And they that know thy ho - ly Name, there - fore shall trust in thee: For thou for - sake,
Bass
With heart and mouth to thee, O Lord, will I sing laud and praise, And speak of all,
Know thou that he who is a - bove for e - ver more shall reign: And in the seat,
And they that know thy ho - ly Name, there - fore shall trust in thee: For thou for - sake,
5
works, thy wond' - rous works and them de - clare al - ways, and them de -
ty, of e - qui - ty true judg - ment will main - tain, true judg - ment
suit, for - sak - est not in their ne - ces - si - ty, in their ne -
works, all thy wond' - rous works and them de - clare al - ways, and them de - clare, and them de -
ty, seat of e - qui - ty true judg - ment will main - tain, true judg - ment will, true judg - ment
suit, thou for - sak - est not in their ne - ces - si - ty, ne - ces - si - ty, in their ne -
speak of all thy wond' - rous works and them de - clare al - ways, and them de -
in the seat of e - qui - ty true judg - ment will main - tain, true judg - ment
thou for - sak - est not their suit in their ne - ces - si - ty, in their ne -
speak of all thy wond' - rous works and them de - clare al - ways, and them de - clare, and them de -
in the seat of e - qui - ty true judg - ment will main - tain, true judg - ment will, true judg - ment
thou for - sak - est not their suit in their ne - ces - si - ty, ne - ces - si - ty, in their ne -
8
clare al - ways.
will main - tain.
ces - si - ty.
clare al - ways. I will be glad and much re - joice
will main - tain. With ju - stice he will keep and guide
ces - si - ty. Sing psalms there - fore un - to the Lord,
clare al - ways. I will be glad, I will be glad and much re -
will main - tain. With ju - stice he, with ju - stice he will keep and
ces - si - ty. Sing psalms there - fore, sing psalms there - fore un - to the
clare al - ways. I will be glad, I will be glad and much re -
will main - tain. With ju - stice he, with ju - stice he will keep and
ces - si - ty. Sing psalms there - fore, sing psalms there - fore un - to the

Original key A

Psalm 18

Thomas Sternhold

Matthew Cooke

10

trust, the wor - ker of my health, My buck - ler, my buck - ler,
me, and bound me e - very - where; The flow - ing the flow - ing
grief did pray to God for grace, And he, and he,

trust, the wor - ker of my health, My buck - ler, my buck - ler, my
me, and bound me e - very - where; The flow - ing the flow - ing, the
grief did pray to God for grace, And he, and he, and

trust, the wor - ker of my health, My buck - ler, my re - fuge, my buck - ler,
me, and bound me e - very - where; The flow - ing, the flow - ing, the flow - ing,
grief did pray to God for grace, And he, and he, and he

trust, the wor - ker of my health, My re - fuge, my buck - ler, my buck - ler,
me, and bound me e - very - where; The flow - ing, the flow - ing, the flow - ing,
grief did pray to God for grace, And he, and he, and he

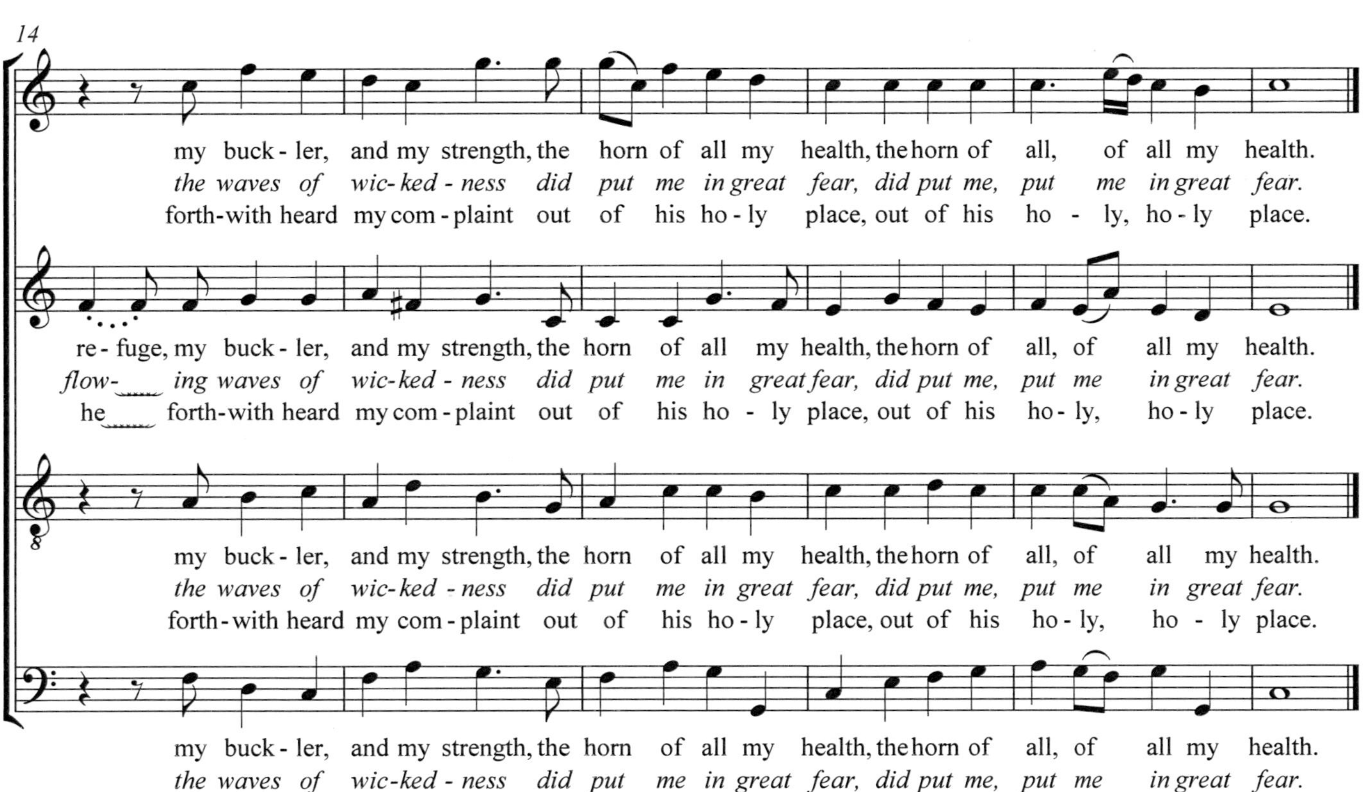

Psalm 21

Thomas Sternhold

Matthew Cooke

7
in thee his Sa - viour. For thou hast giv'n un - to him his
a crown of per - fect gold. And when he ask'd life of thee there-
thou hast u - pon him laid. Thou wilt give him fe - lici - ty that
joice in thee his Sa - viour. For thou hast giv'n un - to him his
head a crown of per - fect gold. And when he ask'd life of thee there -
both thou hast u - pon him laid. Thou wilt give him fe - lici - ty that
in thee his Sa - viour. For thou hast giv'n un - to him, un - to him his
a crown of per - fect gold. And when he ask'd life of thee, life of thee there-
thou hast u - pon him laid. Thou wilt give him, wilt give him fe - lici - ty that
in thee his Sa - viour. For thou hast giv'n, for thou hast giv'n un - to him his
a crown of per - fect gold. And when he ask'd, and when he ask'd life of thee there-
thou hast u - pon him laid. Thou wilt give him, thou wilt give him fe - lici - ty that
11
god - ly heart's de - sire; To him thou no - thing hast de - ny'd, to
of thou mad'st him sure, To have long life, yea such a life, to
ne - ver shall de - cay, And with thy chear - ful coun - te - nance, and
god - ly heart's de - sire; To him thou no - thing hast de - ny'd, to
of thou mad'st him sure, To have long life, yea such a life, to
ne - ver shall de - cay, And with thy chear - ful coun - te - nance, and
god - ly heart's de - sire; To him thou no - thing
of thou mad'st him sure, To have long life, yea
ne - ver shall de - cay, And with thy chear - ful
god - ly heart's de - sire; To him thou no - thing
of thou mad'st him sure, To have long life, yea
ne - ver shall de - cay, And with thy chear - ful
13
him thou no - thing, no - thing hast de - ny'd of that he did re - quire.
have long life, yea such a, such a life as e - ver shall en - dure.
with thy chear - ful, chear - ful coun - te - nance wilt com - fort him al - way.
him thou no - thing, no - thing hast de - ny'd of that he did re - quire.
have long life, yea such a, such a life as e - ver shall en - dure.
with thy chear - ful, chear - ful coun - te - nance wilt com - fort him al - way.
hast de - ny'd, thou no - thing hast de - ny'd of that he did re - quire.
such a life, a life, yea such a life as e - ver shall en - dure.
coun - te - nance, thy chear - ful coun - te - nance wilt com - fort him al - way.
hast de - ny'd, thou no - thing hast de - ny'd of that he did re - quire.
such a life, a life, yea such a life as e - ver shall en - dure.
coun - te - nance, thy chear - ful coun - te - nance wilt com - fort him al - way.

Psalm 23

William Whittingham

Matthew Cooke

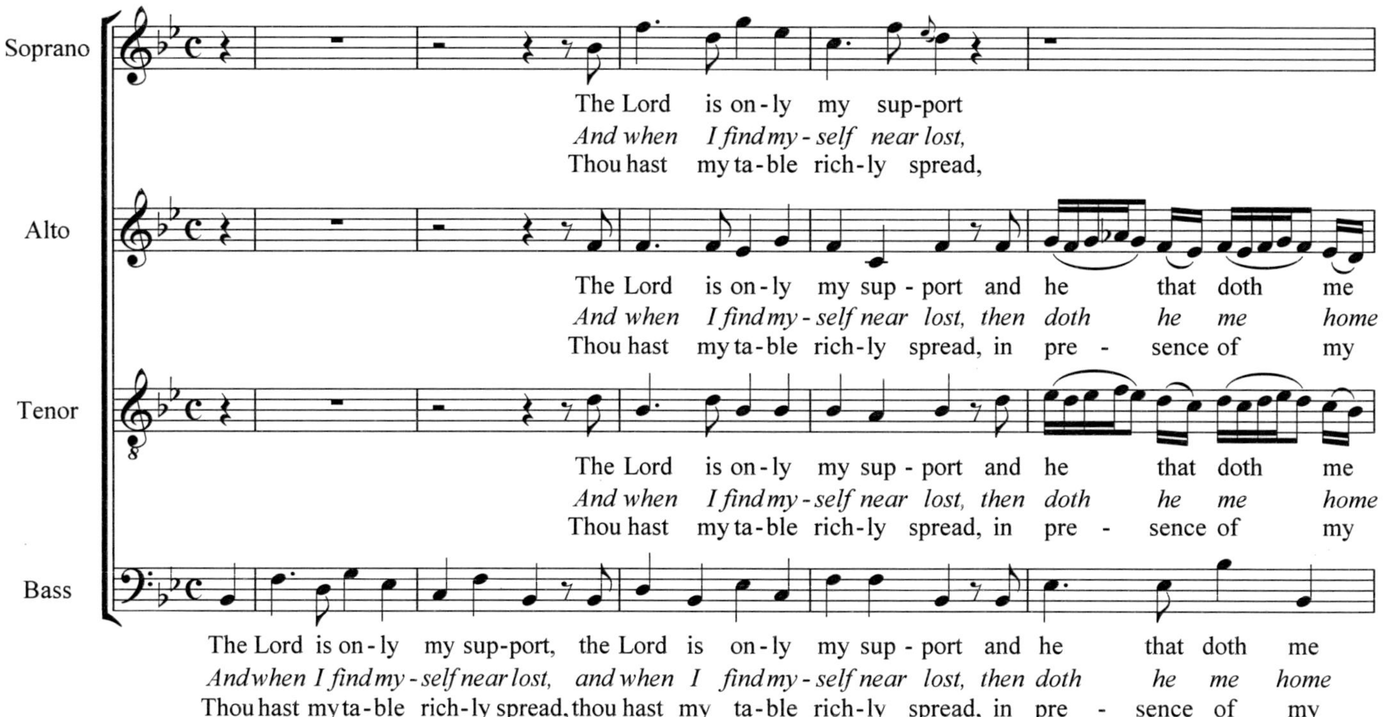

10
stand in need, where - of I stand in need? where
own Name's sake, ev'n for his own Name's sake. yet
o - ver - flow, my cup doth o - ver - flow. thy
stand in need, where-of I stand in need? In pas - tures green he lead - eth me, where
own Name's sake, ev'n for his own Name's sake. And tho' I were ev'n at death's door, yet
o - ver flow, my cup doth o - ver - flow. And fi - nal - ly while breath doth last, thy
stand in need, where-of I stand in need? In pas - tures green he lead - eth me, where
own Name's sake, ev'n for his own Name's sake. And tho' I were ev'n at death's door, yet
o - ver flow, my cup doth o - ver - flow. And fi - nal - ly while breath doth last, thy
stand in need, where-of I stand in need? In pas - tures green he lead - eth me, where
own Name's sake, ev'n for his own Name's sake. And tho' I were ev'n at death's door, yet
o - ver - flow, my cup doth o - ver - flow. And fi - nal - ly while breath doth last, thy
14
I do safe - ly lie, And af - ter
wou'd I fear no ill; For both thy
grace shall me de - fend; And in the
I do safe - ly lie, And af - ter leads, af - ter
wou'd I fear no ill; For both thy rod, both thy
grace shall me de - fend; And in the house, in the
I do safe - ly lie, And af - ter leads, af - ter leads, af - ter
wou'd I fear no ill; For both thy rod, both thy rod, both thy
grace shall me de - fend; And in the house, in the house, in the
I do safe - ly lie, And af - ter leads me to the streams, af - ter
wou'd I fear no ill; For both thy rod and shep - herd's crook, both thy
grace shall me de - fend; And in the house of God will I, in the
17
leads me to the streams which run most plea - sant - ly.
rod and shep - herd's crook af - ford me com - fort still.
house of God will I my life for e - ver spend.
leads me to the streams which run most plea - sant - ly.
rod and shep - herd's crook af - ford me com - fort still.
house of God will I my life for e - ver spend.
leads me to the streams which run most plea - sant - ly.
rod and shep - herd's crook af - ford me com - fort still.
house of God will I my life for e - ver spend.
leads me to the streams which run most plea - sant - ly.
rod and shep - herd's crook af - ford me com - fort still.
house of God will I my life for e - ver spend.

Psalm 29

Thomas Sternhold

Matthew Cooke

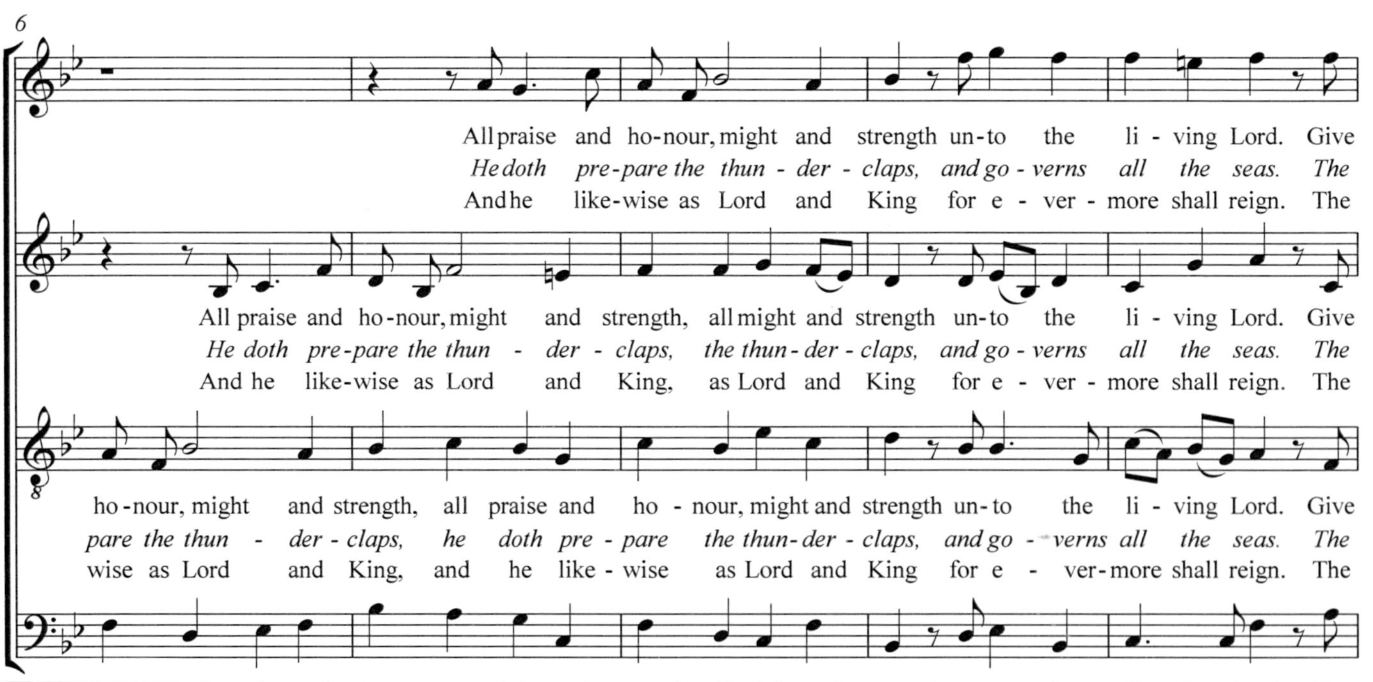

11
glo - ry to his ho - ly Name, and ho - nour him a - lone; Give wor - ship to his Ma - jes -
voice of God is of great force, and won - drous ex - cel - lent; It is most migh - ty in ef -
Lord will give his peo - ple strength, where - by they shall in - crease; And he will bless his cho - sen
glo - ry to his ho - ly Name, and ho - nour him a - lone; Give wor - ship, wor - ship
voice of God is of great force, and won - drous ex - cel - lent; It is most migh - ty
Lord will give his peo - ple strength, where - by they shall in - crease; And he will bless his
glo - ry to his ho - ly Name, and ho - nour him a - lone; Give wor - ship
voice of God is of great force, and won - drous ex - cel - lent; It is most
Lord will give his peo - ple strength, where - by they shall in - crease; And he will
glo - ry to his ho - ly Name, and ho - nour him a - lone; Give
voice of God is of great force, and won - drous ex - cel - lent; It
Lord will give his peo - ple strength, where - by they shall in - crease; And

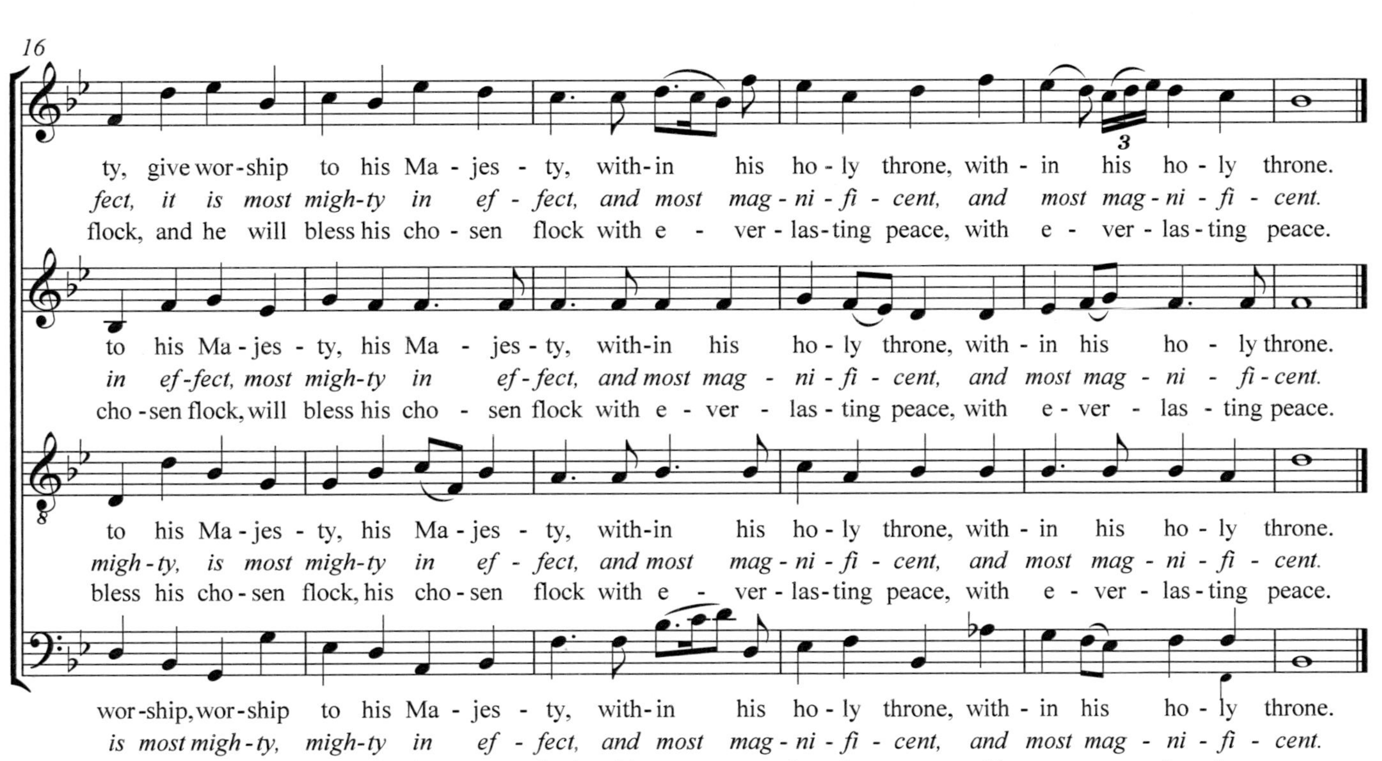
16
ty, give wor - ship to his Ma - jes - ty, with - in his ho - ly throne, with - in his ho - ly throne.
fect, it is most migh - ty in ef - fect, and most mag - ni - fi - cent, and most mag - ni - fi - cent.
flock, and he will bless his cho - sen flock with e - ver - las - ting peace, with e - ver - las - ting peace.
to his Ma - jes - ty, his Ma - jes - ty, with - in his ho - ly throne, with - in his ho - ly throne.
in ef - fect, most migh - ty in ef - fect, and most mag - ni - fi - cent, and most mag - ni - fi - cent.
cho - sen flock, will bless his cho - sen flock with e - ver - las - ting peace, with e - ver - las - ting peace.
to his Ma - jes - ty, his Ma - jes - ty, with - in his ho - ly throne, with - in his ho - ly throne.
migh - ty, is most migh - ty in ef - fect, and most mag - ni - fi - cent, and most mag - ni - fi - cent.
bless his cho - sen flock, his cho - sen flock with e - ver - las - ting peace, with e - ver - las - ting peace.
wor - ship, wor - ship to his Ma - jes - ty, with - in his ho - ly throne, with - in his ho - ly throne.
is most migh - ty, migh - ty in ef - fect, and most mag - ni - fi - cent, and most mag - ni - fi - cent.
he will bless, will bless his cho - sen flock with e - ver - las - ting peace, with e - ver - las - ting peace.

Psalm 30

John Hopkins

Matthew Cooke

9
thee I cry'd in all my pain and grief,
prove and see the good - ness of the Lord,
grief and woe in - to a cheer - ful voice,
thee I cry'd in all my pain and grief,
prove and see the good - ness of the Lord,
grief and woe in - to a cheer - ful voice,
cry'd, I cry'd in all my pain and grief, Thou gav'st an
see, and see the good - ness of the Lord, In ho - nour
woe, and woe in - to a cheer - ful voice My sack-cloth
cry'd, I cry'd in all my pain and grief, Thou gav'st an ear and didst pro -
see, and see the good - ness of the Lord, In ho - nour of his Ma - je -
woe, and woe in - to a cheer - ful voice, My sack-cloth didst take off al -
12
Thou gav'st an ear and didst pro -
In ho - nour of his Ma - je -
My sack - cloth didst take off al -
Thou gav'st an ear, thou gav'st an ear and didst pro -
In ho - nour of, in ho - nour of his Ma - je -
My sack - cloth didst, my sack - cloth didst take off al -
ear and did'st pro - vide, thou gav'st an ear and didst pro -
of his Ma - je - sty, in ho - nour of his Ma - je -
didst take off al - so, my sack - cloth didst take off al -
vide, thou gav'st an ear and did'st pro - vide, and didst pro -
sty, in ho - nour of his Ma - je - sty, his Ma - je -
so, my sack - cloth didst take off al - so, take off al -
14
vide to ease me with re - lief.
sty re - joice with one ac - cord.
so, and mad'st me to re - joice.
vide to ease me with re - lief.
sty re - joice with one ac - cord.
so, and mad'st me to re - joice.
vide to ease me with re - lief.
sty re - joice with one ac - cord.
so, and mad'st me to re - joice.
vide to ease me with re - lief.
sty re - joice with one ac - cord.
so, and mad'st me to re - joice.

Psalm 33

John Hopkins

Matthew Cooke

13
tr
with psal - te - ry; With ten string'd soun - ding in - stru - ments Praise ye the Lord, with
a - bove were wrought; Their hosts and po - wers ev' - ry one His breath to pass, their
eous, right - eous law; And all the world with one ac - cord Dread him and stand, and
with psal - te - ry; With soun - ding in - stru - ments Praise ye the Lord, with
a - bove were wrought; Their po - wers ev' - ry one His breath to pass, their
eous, right - eous law; The world with one ac - cord Dread him and stand, and
19
ten string'd soun - ding in - stru - ments Praise ye the Lord, the Lord most high.
hosts and po - wers ev' - ry one His breath to pass, to pass hath brought.
all the world with one ac - cord Dread him and stand, and stand in awe.

Psalm 46

John Hopkins

Matthew Cooke

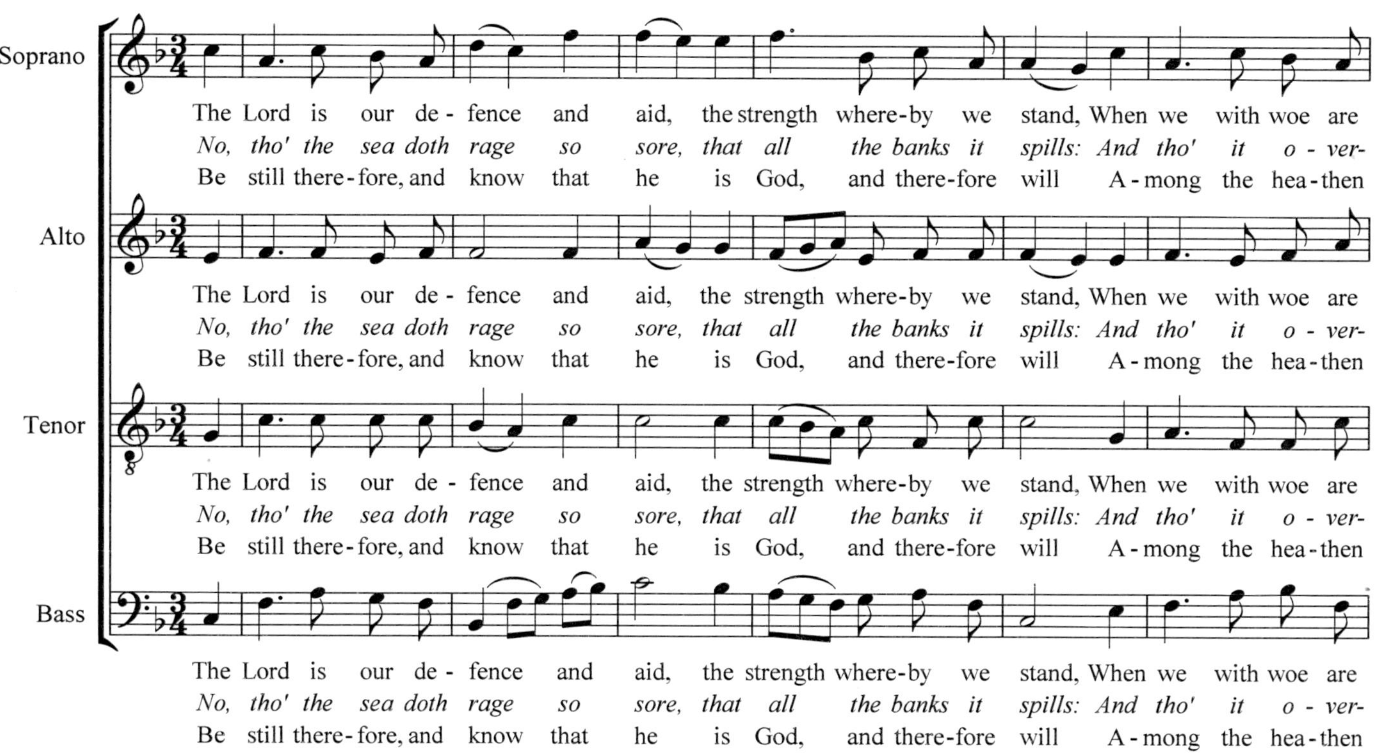

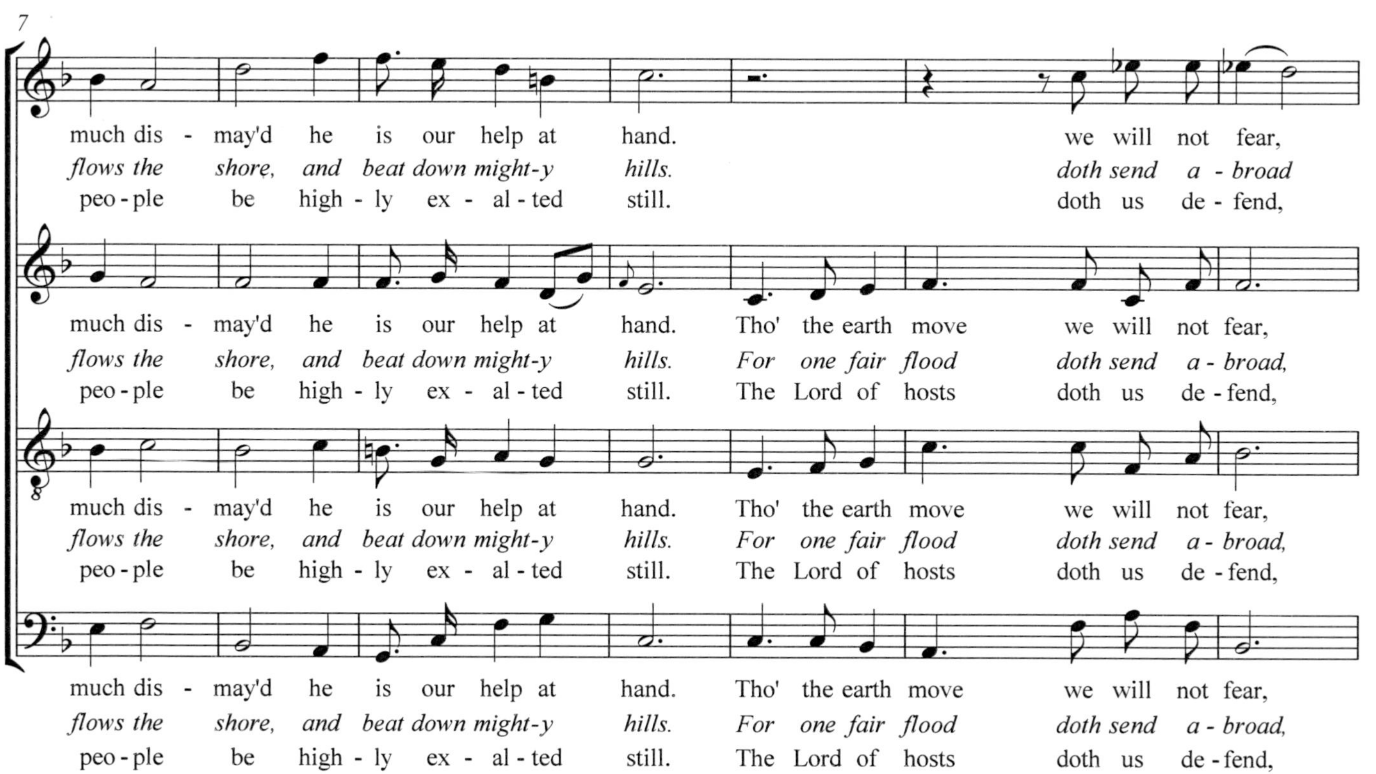

14
we will not fear tho' moun-tains high and steep
doth send a - broad his plea - sant streams a - pace:
doth us de - fend, he is our strength and tow'r;
tho' the earth move we will not fear tho' moun-tains high and steep
for one fair flood doth send a-broad his plea - sant streams a - pace;
the Lord of hosts doth us de-fend, he is our strength and tow'r;
tho' the earth move we will not fear tho' moun-tains high and steep Be
for one fair flood doth send a-broad his plea - sant streams a - pace; To
the Lord of hosts doth us de-fend, he is our strength and tow'r; On
tho' the earth move we will not fear tho' moun-tains high and steep Be thrust and hurl-ed here and
for one fair flood doth send a-broad his plea - sant streams a - pace; To glad the ci - ty of our
the Lord of hosts doth us de-fend, he is our strength and tow'r; On Ja - cob's God we do de-
20
Be thrust and hurl - ed here and
To glad the ci - ty of our
On Ja - cob's God we do de -
Be thrust and hurl - ed here and there, be hurl - ed here and
To glad the ci - ty of our God, the ci - ty of our
On Ja - cob's God we do de - pend, on Ja - cob's God de -
thrust and hurl - ed here and there, here and there, hurl - ed here and
glad the ci - ty of our God, of our God, ci - ty of our
Ja - cob's God we do de - pend, do de - pend, Ja - cob's God we
there, here and there, be
God, of our God, to
pend, do de - pend, on
23
there, here and there with - in the sea so deep.
God, of our God, and wash his ho - ly place.
pend, do de - pend, and on his migh - ty pow'r.
there, here and there with - in the sea so deep.
God, of our God, and wash his ho - ly place.
pend, do de - pend, and on his migh - ty pow'r.
there, be hurl - ed here and there with - in the sea so deep.
God, the ci - ty of our God, and wash his ho - ly place.
do de - pend, we do de - pend, and on his migh - ty pow'r.
thrust and hurl - ed here and there with - in the sea so deep.
glad the ci - ty of our God, and wash his ho - ly place.
Ja - cob's God we do de - pend, and on his migh - ty pow'r.

Psalm 47

John Hopkins

Matthew Cooke

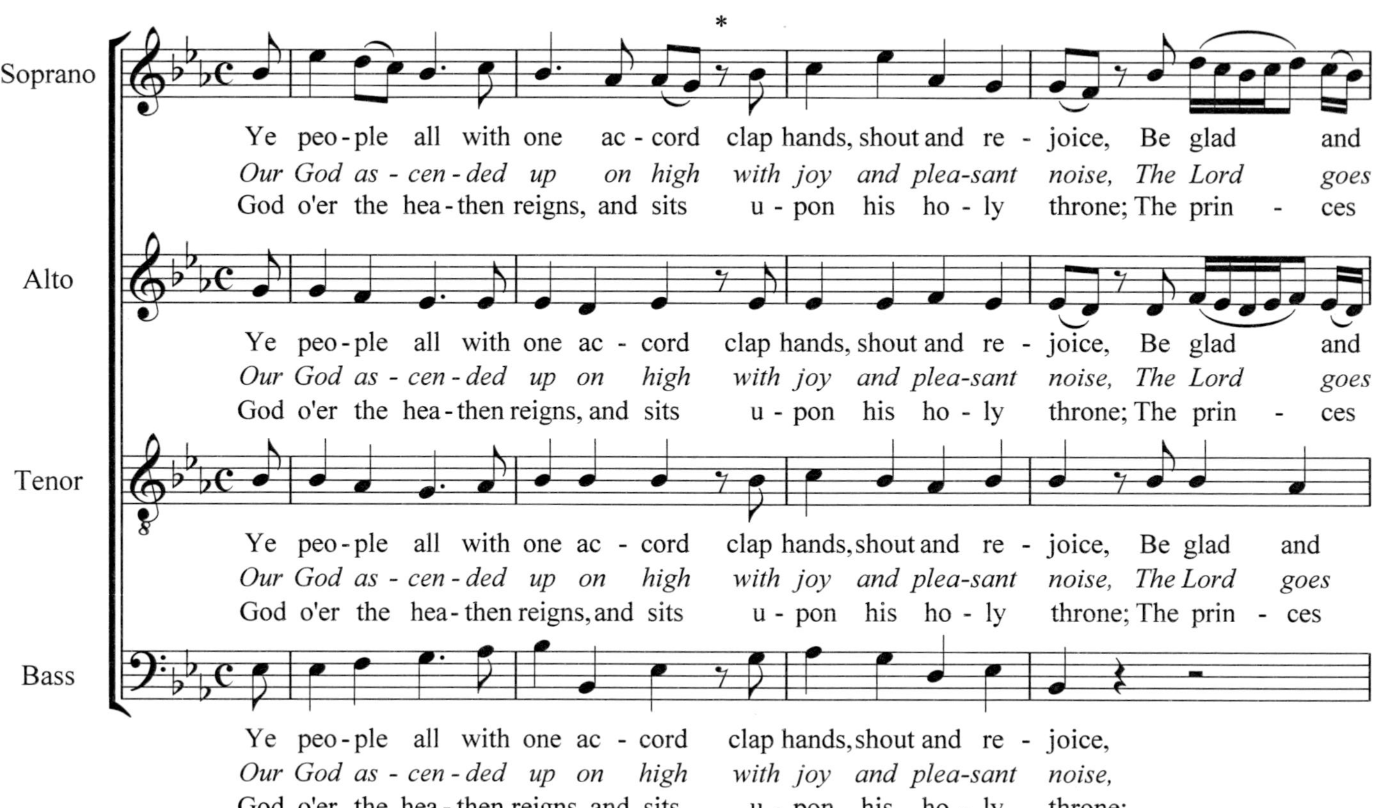

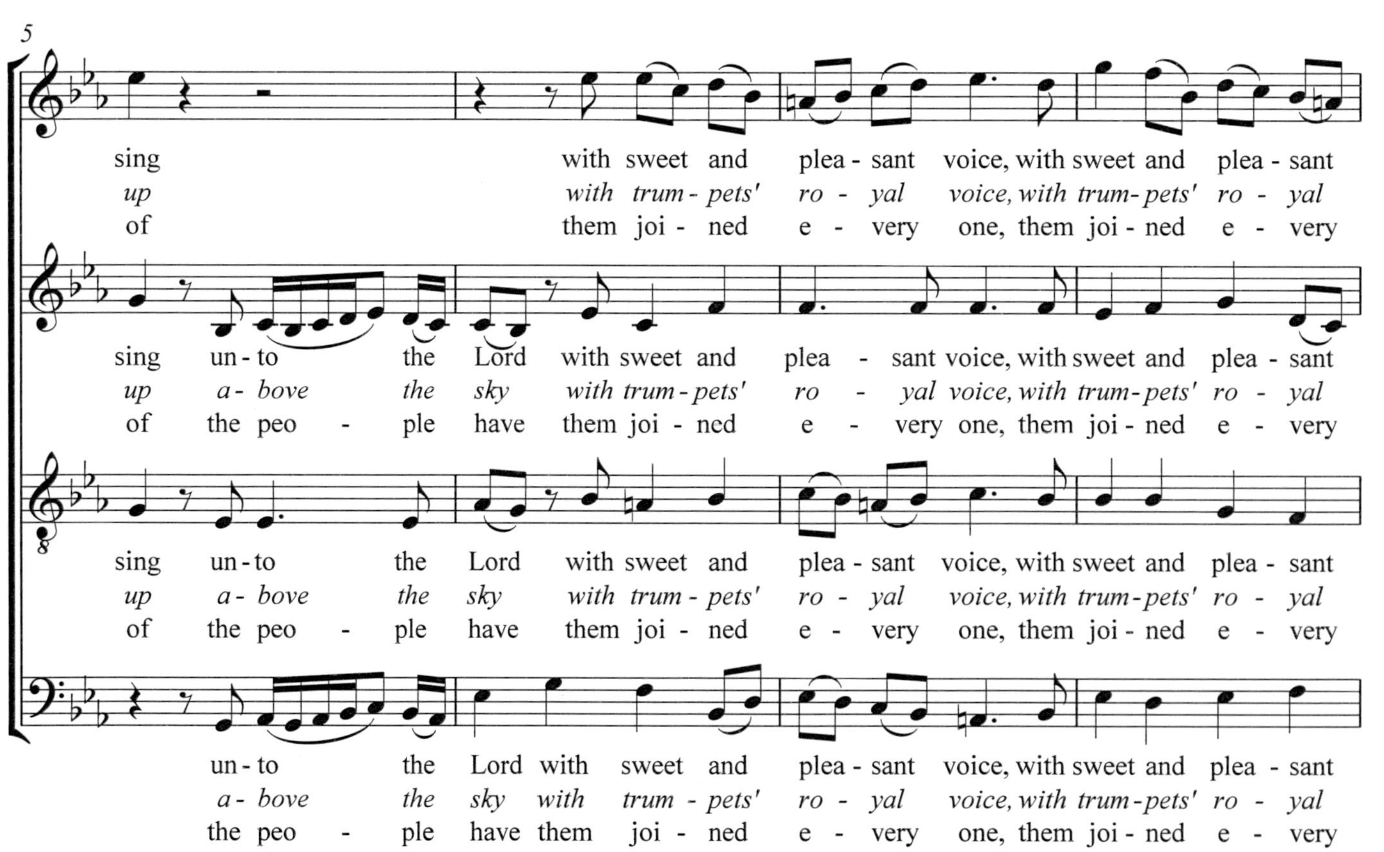

* *Omit the rest in verse 3*

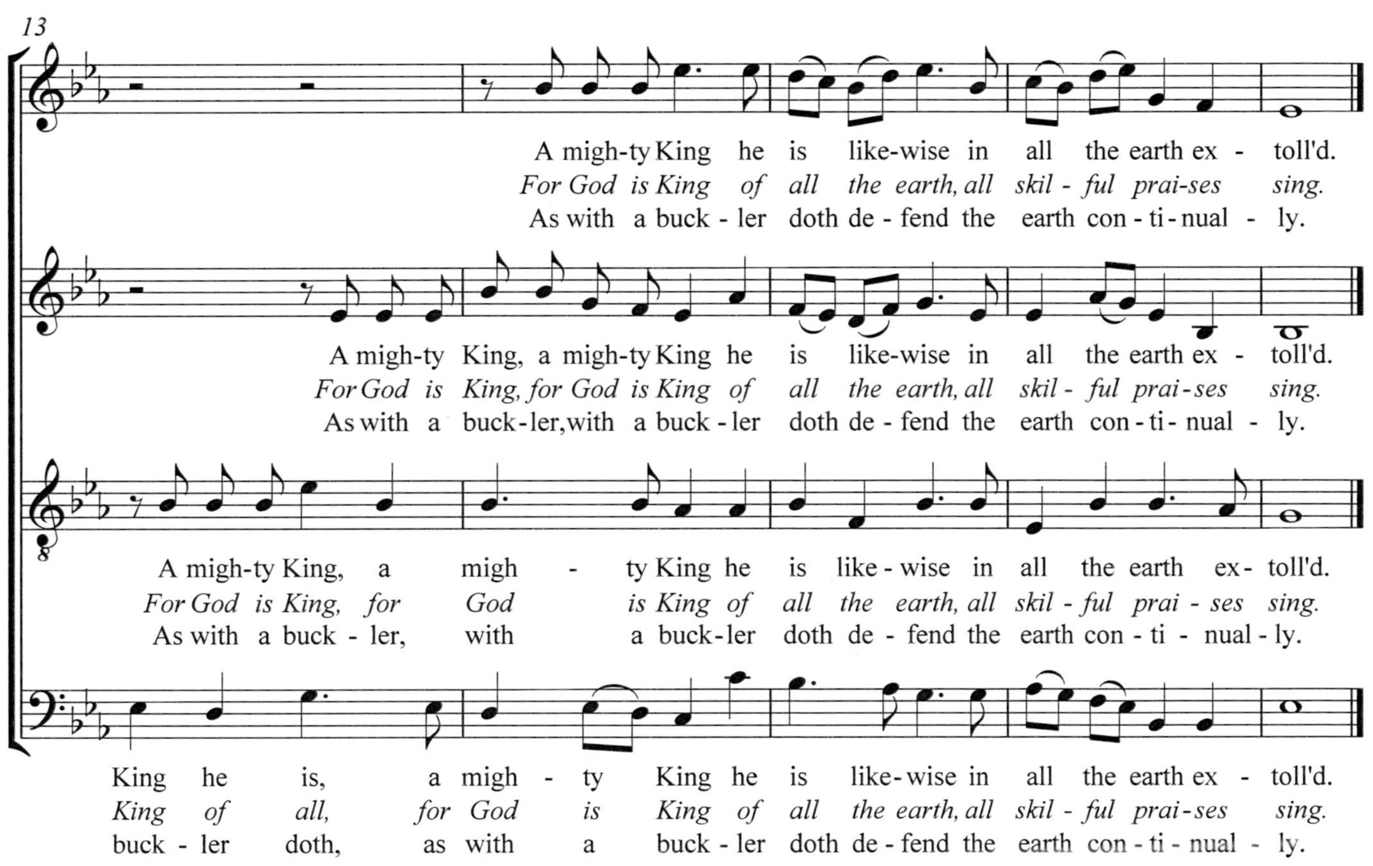

Original key E

Psalm 48

John Hopkins

Matthew Cooke

* *Omit the rest in verse 2.*

11
all the land; The ci - ty of the migh - ty King on her north side doth
full with joys, Al - so of Ju - dah grant, O Lord, the daugh - ters to re -
more is he, And un - to death we are re - solved our guide he still shall
all the land; The ci - ty of the migh - ty King on her north side doth
full with joys, Al - so of Ju - dah grant, O Lord, the daugh - ters to re -
more is he, And un - to death we are re - solved our guide he still shall
all the land; The ci - ty of the migh - ty King on her north side doth
full with joys, Al - so of Ju - dah grant, O Lord, the daugh - ters to re -
more is he, And un - to death we are re - solved our guide he still shall
15
The ci - ty
Al - so of
And un - to
stand, the ci - ty of the might - y
joice, al - so of Ju - dah grant, of
be, and un - to death we are re -
stand, the ci - ty of the might - y King, the ci - ty
joice, al - so of Ju - dah grant, O Lord, al - so of
be, and un - to death we are re - solved, and un - to
stand, the ci - ty of the might - y King, the ci - ty of the might - y
joice, al - so of Ju - dah grant, O Lord, al - so of Ju - dah grant, of
be, and un - to death we are re - solved, and un - to death we are re -
17
of the might - y King on her north side doth stand.
Ju - dah grant, O Lord, the daugh - ters to re - joice.
death we are re - solved our guide he still shall be.
King, the might - y King on her north side doth stand.
Ju - dah grant, O Lord, the daugh - ters to re - joice.
solved, we are re - solved our guide he still shall be.
of the might - y King on her north side doth stand.
Ju - dah grant, O Lord, the daugh - ters to re - joice.
death we are re - solved our guide he still shall be.
King, the might - y King on her north side doth stand.
Ju - dah grant, O Lord, the daugh - ters to re - joice.
solved, we are re - solved our guide he still shall be.

Thomas Norton

Psalm 105

Matthew Cooke

15
yea, sing un - to him praise;
of his e - ter - nal might,
his ser - vant are the seed,
joy - ful - ly un - to the Lord, yea, sing un - to him praise; And talk of all his won - d'rous
ye the Lord, and seek the strength of his e - ter - nal might, Yea, seek his face in - ces - sant-
that of faith - ful A - bra - ham his ser - vant are the seed, Ye his e - lect, the chil - dren
joy - ful - ly un - to the Lord, yea, sing un - to him praise; And talk of
ye the Lord, and seek the strength of his e - ter - nal might, Yea, seek his
that of faith - ful A - bra - ham his ser - vant are the seed, Ye his e -
joy - ful - ly un - to the Lord, yea, sing un - to him praise;
ye the Lord, and seek the strength of his e - ter - nal might,
that of faith - ful A - bra - ham his ser - vant are the seed,
20
And talk of all his won - d'rous works, his won - d'rous
Yea, seek his face _ in - ces - sant - ly, in - ces - sant -
Ye his e - lect, _ the chil - dren that, the chil - dren
works, and talk of all his won - d'rous works, his won - d'rous
ly, — yea, seek his face in - ces - sant - ly, in - ces - sant -
that, ye his e - lect, the chil - dren that, the chil - dren
all his won - d'rous works, and talk of all his won - d'rous
face in - ces - sant - ly, yea, seek his face in - ces - sant -
lect, the chil - dren that, ye his e - lect, the chil - dren
And talk of all his won - d'rous works, his won - d'rous
Yea, seek his face in - ces - sant - ly, in - ces - sant -
Ye his e - lect, the chil - dren that, the chil - dren
23
works that he hath wrought al - ways, that he hath wrought al - ways.
ly, and pre - sence of his sight, and pre - sence of his sight.
that of Ja - cob do pro - ceed, of Ja - cob do pro - ceed.
works that he hath wrought al - ways, that he hath wrought al - ways.
ly, and pre - sence of his sight, and pre - sence of his sight.
that of Ja - cob do pro - ceed, of Ja - cob do pro - ceed.
works that he hath wrought al - ways, that he hath wrought al - ways.
ly, and pre - sence of his sight, and pre - sence of his sight.
that of Ja - cob do pro - ceed, of Ja - cob do pro - ceed.
works that he hath wrought al - ways, that he hath wrought al - ways.
ly, and pre - sence of his sight, and pre - sence of his sight.
that of Ja - cob do pro - ceed, of Ja - cob do pro - ceed.

[Anthem on] Psalm 137

William Whittingham

Matthew Cooke

20
songs and plea - sant, plea - sant me - lo - dy. A - las! said we, who can once frame his hea - vy
songs and plea - sant, plea - sant me - lo - dy. A - las! said we, who can once frame his hea - vy
songs and plea - sant, plea - sant me - lo - dy. A - las! said we, who can once frame his hea - vy
25
tr
heart to sing The prai - ses of our liv - ing God, thus un-der a strange king? But yet if
heart to sing The prai - ses of our liv - ing God, thus un-der a strange king? But yet if
heart to sing The prai - ses of our liv - ing God, thus un-der a strange king? But yet if
30
I Je - ru - sa - lem out of my heart let slide; Then let my fin-gers quite for - get the
I Je - ru - sa - lem out of my heart let slide; Then let my fin - gers quite for - get the
I Je - ru - sa - lem out of my heart let slide; Then let my fin - gers quite for - get the
35
war - bling harp to guide: And let my tongue with-in my mouth be ty'd for-
war - bling harp to guide: And let my tongue with-in my mouth be ty'd for -
war - bling harp to guide: And let my tongue with-in my mouth be ty'd for -
39
ev - er fast, If I re-joice be - fore I see thy full de - li - v'rance
ev - er fast, If I re - joice be - fore I see thy full de - li - v'rance
ev - er fast, If I re - joice be - fore I see thy full de - li - v'rance

Chorus
Soprano
Alto
Tenor
Bass
There-fore, O Lord, re-mem-ber now the cur-sed noise and cry That E - dom's sons a-
past. There-fore, O Lord, re-mem-ber now the cur-sed noise and cry That E-dom's sons a -
past. There-fore, O Lord, re-mem-ber now the cur-sed noise and cry That E-dom's sons a-
past. There-fore, O Lord, re-mem-ber now the cur-sed noise and cry That E-dom's sons a -
48
gainst us brought when they raz'd our ci - ty. Re-mem-ber, Lord, their cru-el words, when with a
gainst us brought when they raz'd our ci - ty. Re-mem-ber, Lord, their cru-el words, when with a
gainst us brought when they raz'd our ci - ty. Re-mem-ber, Lord, their cru-el words, when with a
gainst us brought when they raz'd our ci - ty. Re-mem-ber, Lord, their cru-el words, when with a
53
migh - ty sound They cried, down with it,
migh - ty sound They cried, down with it,
migh - ty sound They cried, down with it,
migh - ty sound They
57
down with it un - to the ve - ry ground. Ev'n so shalt thou, O Ba - by-
down with it un - to the ve - ry ground. Ev'n so shalt thou, O Ba - by-
down with it un - to the ve - ry ground. Ev'n so shalt thou, O Ba - by -
cried, down with it, down with it un - to the ve - ry ground. Ev'n so shalt thou, O Ba - by -

61
lon, at length to dust be brought; And hap-py shall that man be call'd that our re -
lon, at length to dust be brought; And hap-py shall that man be call'd that our re -
lon, at length to dust be brought; And hap-py shall that man be call'd that our re -
lon, at length to dust be brought; And hap-py shall that man be call'd that our re -
65
venge hath wrought; Yea bless - ed shall that man be call'd that takes thy lit - tle
venge hath wrought; Yea bless - ed shall that man be call'd that takes thy lit - tle
venge hath wrought; Yea bless - ed shall that man be call'd that takes thy lit - tle
venge hath wrought; Yea bless - ed shall that man be call'd that takes thy lit - tle
69
ones, And dash - eth them in piec - es small, and dash - eth them in
ones, And dash - eth them in pie - ces small, dash-eth them in
ones And dash - eth them in pie - ces small, in
ones And dash - eth them in pie - ces
72
pie - ces small a-gainst the ve - ry stones, a - gainst the ve - ry, ve - ry stones.
pie - ces small a-gainst the ve - ry stones, a - gainst the ve - ry, ve - ry stones.
pie - ces small a-gainst the ve - ry stones, a - gainst the ve - ry, ve - ry stones.
small a - gainst the ve - ry, ve - ry stones, a - gainst the ve - ry, ve - ry stones.

Hymn for Christmas Day (1): The Day Spring

Ann Murry

Matthew Cooke

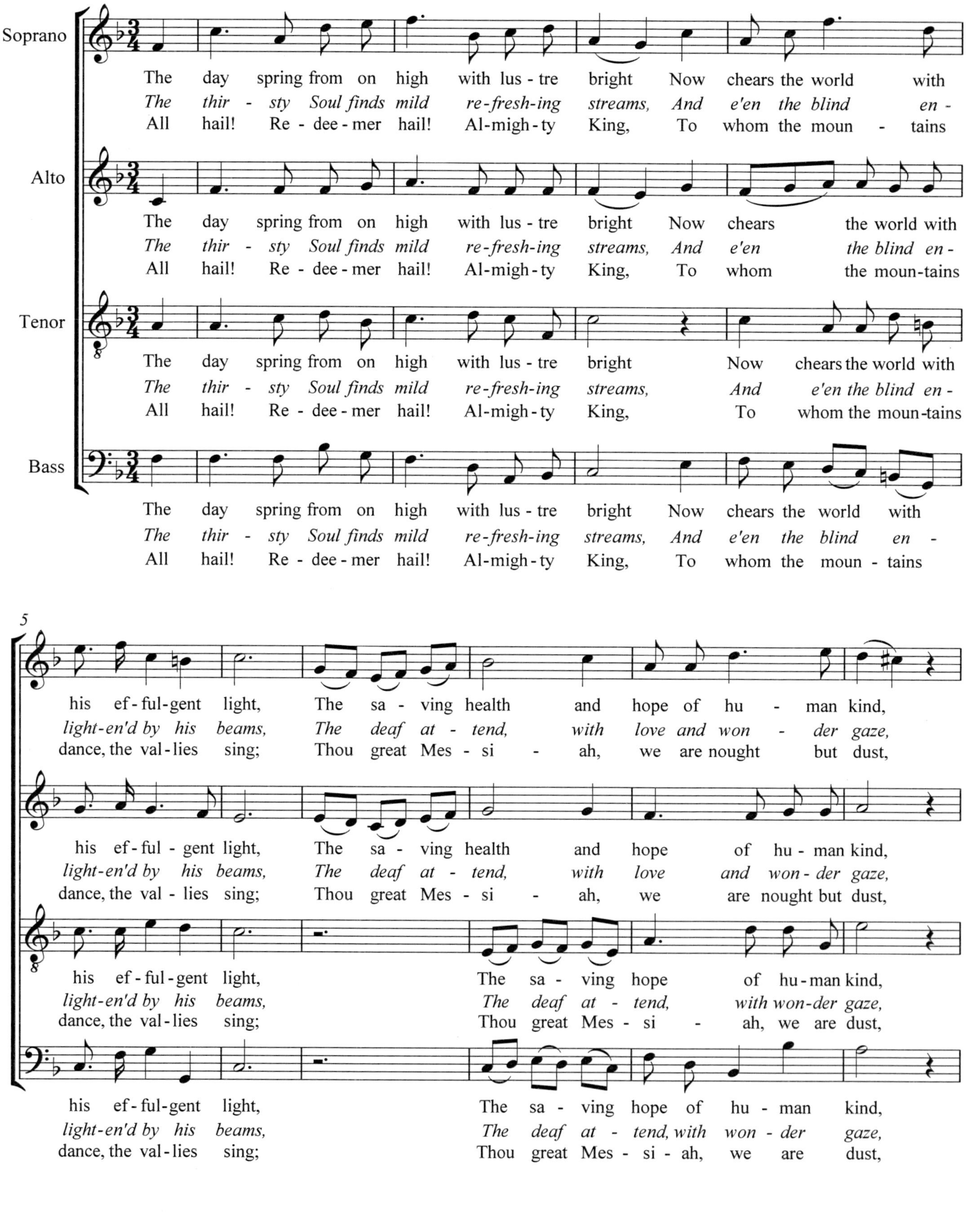

Soprano

The day spring from on high with lus - tre bright Now cheers the world with
The thir - sty Soul finds mild re-fresh-ing streams, And e'en the blind en -
All hail! Re - dee - mer hail! Al-migh - ty King, To whom the moun - tains

Alto

The day spring from on high with lus - tre bright Now cheers the world with
The thir - sty Soul finds mild re-fresh-ing streams, And e'en the blind en -
All hail! Re - dee - mer hail! Al-migh - ty King, To whom the moun-tains

Tenor

The day spring from on high with lus - tre bright Now cheers the world with
The thir - sty Soul finds mild re-fresh-ing streams, And e'en the blind en -
All hail! Re - dee - mer hail! Al-migh - ty King, To whom the moun-tains

Bass

The day spring from on high with lus - tre bright Now cheers the world with
The thir - sty Soul finds mild re-fresh-ing streams, And e'en the blind en -
All hail! Re - dee - mer hail! Al-migh - ty King, To whom the moun - tains

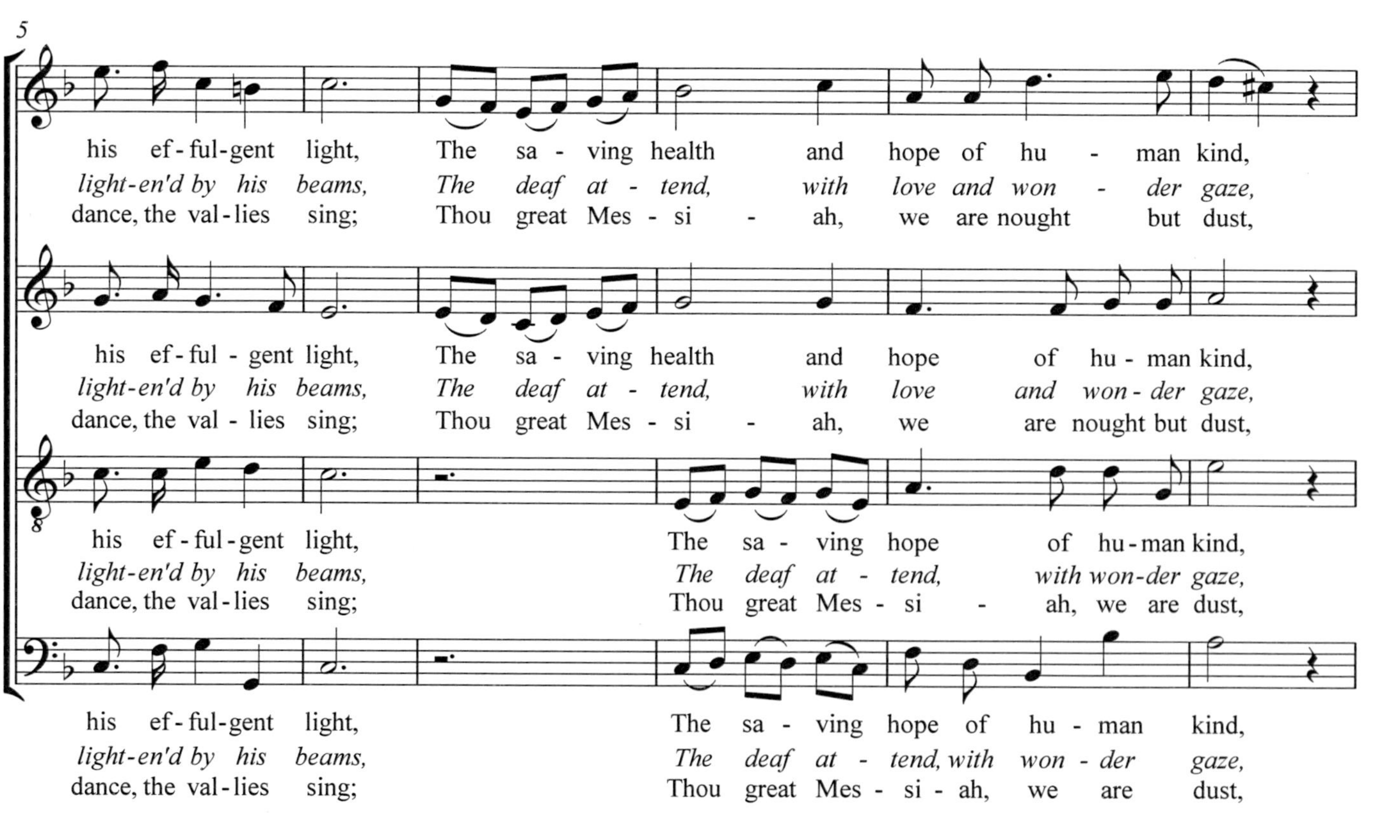

11
Sweet balm of com - fort to the trou-bled mind; The hea - vy la - den
The dumb break forth to sing his might-y praise, At his ap - proach pale
Tho' heirs with thee in king-doms of the just: Ce - le - stial pow'r, of
Sweet balm of com - fort to the trou-bled mind; The hea - vy la - den
The dumb break forth to sing his might-y praise, At his ap - proach pale
Tho' heirs with thee in king-doms of the just: Ce - le - stial pow'r, of
Sweet balm of com - fort, of com-fort to the trou - bled mind; The hea - vy la - den
The dumb break forth, dumb break forth to sing his might - y praise, At his ap - proach pale
Tho' heirs with thee, heirs with thee in king - doms of the just: Ce - le - stial pow'r, of
Sweet balm of com-fort to the trou-bled mind; The hea - vy la - den
The dumb break forth to sing his might-y praise, At his ap - proach pale
Tho' heirs with thee in king - doms of the just: Ce - le - stial pow'r, of

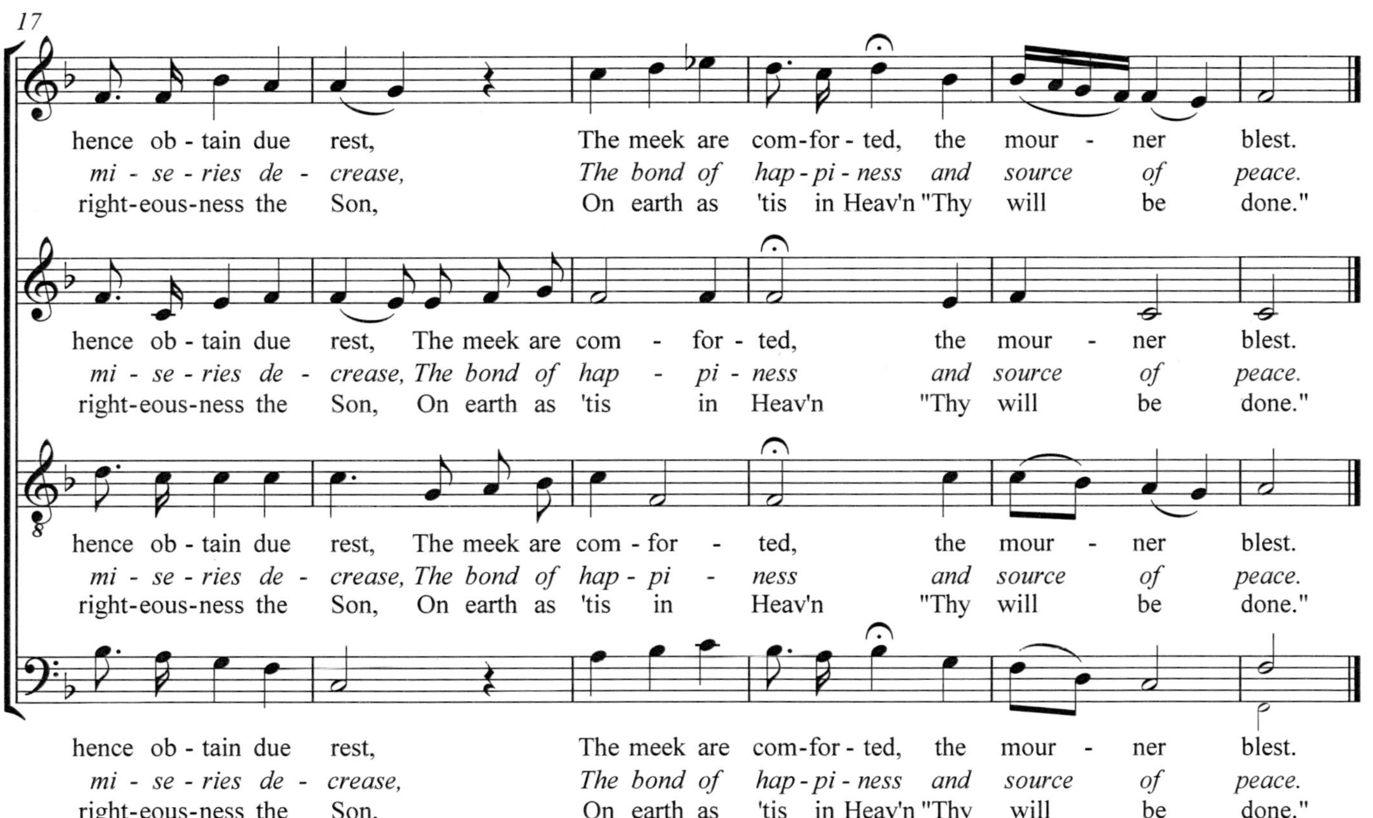
17
hence ob - tain due rest, The meek are com-for - ted, the mour - ner blest.
mi - se - ries de - crease, The bond of hap - pi - ness and source of peace.
right-eous-ness the Son, On earth as 'tis in Heav'n "Thy will be done."
hence ob - tain due rest, The meek are com - for - ted, the mour - ner blest.
mi - se - ries de - crease, The bond of hap - pi - ness and source of peace.
right-eous-ness the Son, On earth as 'tis in Heav'n "Thy will be done."
hence ob - tain due rest, The meek are com - for - ted, the mour - ner blest.
mi - se - ries de - crease, The bond of hap - pi - ness and source of peace.
right-eous-ness the Son, On earth as 'tis in Heav'n "Thy will be done."
hence ob - tain due rest, The meek are com-for - ted, the mour - ner blest.
mi - se - ries de - crease, The bond of hap - pi - ness and source of peace.
right-eous-ness the Son, On earth as 'tis in Heav'n "Thy will be done."

Nahum Tate
Hymn for Christmas Day (2): While Shepherds Watched
Matthew Cooke
Soprano
While shep - herds watched their flocks by night all seat - ed on the
To you in Da - vid's town this day is born of Da - vid's
Thus spake the Se - raph, and forth - with ap - pear'd a shi - ning
Alto
While shep - herds watched their flocks by night all seat - ed on the
To you in Da - vid's town this day is born of Da - vid's
Thus spake the Se - raph, and forth - with ap - pear'd a shi - ning
Tenor
While shep - herds watched their flocks by night all seat - ed on the
To you in Da - vid's town this day is born of Da - vid's
Thus spake the Se - raph, and forth - with ap - pear'd a shi - ning
Bass
While shep - herds watched their flocks by night all seat - ed on the
To you in Da - vid's town this day is born of Da - vid's
Thus spake the Se - raph, and forth - with ap - pear'd a shi - ning
4
ground The An - gel of the Lord came down and glo - ry
line The Sa - viour, who is Christ the Lord, and this shall
throng Of An - gels, prai - sing God, and thus ad - dress'd their
ground The An - gel of the Lord came down and glo - ry shone, glo - ry
line The Sa - viour, who is Christ the Lord, and this shall be, this shall
throng Of An - gels, prai - sing God, and thus ad-dress'd their joy - ful, their
ground The An - gel of the Lord came down and glo - ry
line The Sa - viour, who is Christ the Lord, and this shall
throng Of An - gels, prai - sing God, and thus ad - dress'd their
ground The An - gel of the Lord came down and glo - ry shone, and glo - ry
line The Sa - viour, who is Christ the Lord, and this shall be, and this shall
throng Of An - gels, prai - sing God, and thus ad-dress'd their joy, ad - dress'd their
7
shone a - round. Fear not said he for migh - ty dread had seiz'd their trou - bled
be a sign: The heav'n-ly Babe you there shall find to hu - man view dis -
joy - ful song: All glo - ry be to God on high, and to the earth be
shone a - round. Fear not said he for migh - ty dread had seiz'd their trou - bled
be a sign: The heav'n-ly Babe you there shall find to hu - man view dis -
joy - ful song: All glo - ry be to God on high, and to the earth be
shone a - round. Fear not said he for migh - ty dread, migh - ty dread had seiz'd their trou - bled
be a sign: The heav'n-ly Babe you there shall find, there shall find to hu - man view dis -
joy - ful song: All glo - ry be to God on high, God on high, and to the earth be
shone a - round. Fear not said he for migh - ty dread had seiz'd their trou - bled
be a sign: The heav'n - ly Babe you there shall find to hu - man view dis -
joy - ful song: All glo - ry be to God on high, and to the earth be

11
mind: Glad ti-dings of great joy I bring to you and
play'd, All mean-ly wrapt in swa-thing bands, and in a
peace; Good-will hence-forth from heav'n to men be-gin, and
mind: Glad ti-dings of great joy I bring, glad ti-dings of great joy I bring to you and
play'd, All mean-ly wrapt in swa-thing bands, all mean-ly wrapt in swa-thing bands, and in a
peace; Good-will hence-forth from heav'n to men, good-will hence-forth from heav'n to men be-gin, and
mind: Glad ti-dings of great joy I bring, glad ti-dings of great joy I bring to you and
play'd, All mean-ly wrapt in swa-thing bands, all mean-ly wrapt in swa-thing bands, and in a
peace; Good-will hence-forth from heav'n to men, good-will hence-forth from heav'n to men be-gin, and
mind: Glad ti-dings of great joy I bring to you and
play'd, All mean-ly wrapt in swa-thing bands, and in a
peace; Good-will hence-forth from heav'n to men be-gin, and
14
all man-kind, glad
man-ger laid, all
ne-ver cease, good-
all man-kind, glad ti-dings of great joy I bring
man-ger laid, all mean-ly wrapt in swa-thing bands,
ne-ver cease, good-will hence-forth from heav'n to men
all man-kind, glad ti-dings of great joy I bring, glad
man-ger laid, all mean-ly wrapt in swa-thing bands, all
ne-ver cease, good-will hence-forth from heav'n to men, good-
all man-kind, glad ti-dings of great joy I bring, glad
man-ger laid, all mean-ly wrapt in swa-thing bands, all
ne-ver cease, good-will hence-forth from heav'n to men, good-
16
ti-dings of great joy I bring to you and all man-kind.
mean-ly wrapt in swa-thing bands, and in a man-ger laid.
will hence-forth from heav'n to men be-gin, and ne-ver cease.
to you and all man-kind.
and in a man-ger laid.
be-gin, and ne-ver cease.
ti-dings of great joy I bring to you and all man-kind.
mean-ly wrapt in swa-thing bands, and in a man-ger laid.
will hence-forth from heav'n to men be-gin, and ne-ver cease.
ti-dings of great joy I bring to you and all man-kind.
mean-ly wrapt in swa-thing bands, and in a man-ger laid.
will hence-forth from heav'n to men be-gin, and ne-ver cease.
Original key A

Keyboard reductions

These are included for the benefit of choirs that use a keyboard instrument for rehearsal or accompaniment. Soprano and tenor parts are written stems up, alto and bass stems down (except in a few alto passages where the soprano part rests). It will be noticed that the bass and tenor parts frequently cross, so the bass part should be reinforced where possible *(see page 26)**.*

Psalm 9

Psalm 18
5
9
13
16

Psalm 21

Psalm 23

Psalm 29

Psalm 30

Psalm 33 (instrumental notes omitted)

Psalm 46

Psalm 47

* *Omit the rest in verse 3*

Psalm 48

* *Omit the rest in verse 2*

Psalm 105 (instrumental notes omitted)

[Anthem on] Psalm 137
Verse for 3 Voices (A,T,B)

28
tr
32
36
40
Chorus
44
48

52
57
61
65
69
72

Hymn for Christmas Day (1): The Day Spring

Hymn for Christmas Day (2): While Shepherds Watched

ND - #0277 - 080726 - C0 - 297/210/7 - PB - 9781784563509 - Gloss Lamination